The
Book
of
Eros

The Book of Eros

Arts and Letters from *Yellow Silk*

Edited by Lily Pond and Richard Russo

Crown Trade Paperbacks

Copyright © 1995 by Lily Pond and Richard Russo

Published by Crown Trade Paperbacks, 201 East 50th Street,
New York, New York 10022. Member of the Crown Publishing Group.

For more information on Yellow Silk: Journal of Erotic Arts, please contact
Yellow Silk, P.O. Box 6374, Albany, California 94706.

Originally published in hardcover by Harmony Books,
a division of Crown Publishers, Inc., in 1995.

Random House, Inc. New York, Toronto, London, Sydney, Auckland

CROWN TRADE PAPERBACKS and colophon are trademarks of Crown Publishers, Inc.

Printed in the United States of America

Design by Nancy Kenmore

Library of Congress Cataloging-in-Publication Data

The book of Eros: arts and letters from Yellow silk / edited by Lily Pond and Richard A. Russo.—1st ed.
        1. Erotic literature, American.   2. American literature—20th century.   I. Pond, Lily.   II. Russo, Richard A. (Richard Anthony), 1946– .   III. Series: Yellow silk.
            PS509.E7B66   1995
            810.8′03538—dc20   94-33164
                                                                                  CIP

ISBN 0-517-88612-X

10   9   8   7   6   5   4   3   2   1

First Paperback Edition

$\mathscr{C}$ontents

𝒮pirits

𝒮elected Orgasms

Wonderland

Divinity

*P*rospects of Joy

$\mathscr{I}$ntroduction

The Book of Eros is a sequel to *Yellow Silk: Erotic Arts and Letters,* which was published in 1991. Like its predecessor, *The Book of Eros* contains our choices from *Yellow Silk* journal, drawn mostly from work published since the first book was compiled four years ago.

When Lily Pond began publishing *Yellow Silk* back in the early 1980s, there were no other journals or anthologies of erotic literature. In part thanks to her trailblazing, that is no longer the case. Today there are many erotic journals, but *Yellow Silk* continues to differ significantly from most of them.

Yellow Silk is first and foremost a *literary* journal, with the unusual aim of seeking to expand our understanding of the erotic. Most of what is published as erotic elsewhere accepts without question the total identification of the erotic with the sexual. Most focus on the "edge"—on being as daring and controversial and titillating as possible, challenging the boundaries of taste rather than of our understanding. *Yellow Silk* is, in fact, more radical than that, because it dares to challenge the underlying assumption that the erotic is only the sexual, and offers a new vision of Eros that goes far beyond genital sex.

What is this new vision of Eros? We have no easy answer. The deeper we look, the more complex it becomes; perhaps there are as many answers as there are human beings. Eros is sexuality, creativity, spirituality—the human longing to touch and be touched, the soul's longing to know and be known, and the body's desire to join with another body; Eros is all these myriad forms of the impulse to reach beyond the Self. No wonder Sappho called him a "limb-loosening, bitter-sweet, impractical wild beast," an insight echoed by Mary Mackey in our opening essay.

The mystery of Eros ultimately may be the mystery of what it means to be fully human. To ask what the erotic is or might be is to ask what human beings are or might be. In that spirit, we offer this collection of provocative, moving, and sometimes beautiful, sometimes disturbing attempts to explore that mystery.

Jane Hirshfield

Half-sleeping,
my body pulls toward yours—
desire a long oar dipping
again and again
in this night's dark rain.

Reflections on Eros and Perfection

Mary Mackey

It's ten fifty-nine in Munich and the famous glockenspiel is about to ring. Tourists packed twenty deep juggle for position, craning their necks to get a better view of the bell tower. Tilting back their heads like a flock of drinking chickens, they aim cameras and binoculars at the motionless figures of the mechanical Queen and King who are perched at the top of the cathedral staring glassily at the bank across the street.

At exactly eleven o'clock the bells begin to chime and the glockenspiel grinds into motion. Wooden courtiers appear out of nowhere and make their bows; wooden knights on wooden horses joust for the royal pleasure; a wooden jester performs tricks; wooden Zouaves in bright red pantaloons dance in a perfect circle, their arms all raised at exactly the same angle.

For hundreds of years the glockenspiel has symbolized the ideal social order, Plato's republic, the Renaissance Great Chain of Being, that final union of church and state, spirit and mind in which each social class moves harmoniously with the rest, a world in which there is no disorder or surprise, only the tidy, eternal peace of complete mechanical predictability.

There is a side to us that loves such perfection and rejoices in such order. The merry-go-round and the wristwatch, the computer and the robot are all cousins of the glockenspiel, as are sonnets, the paintings in the Sistine Chapel, the glossy geometric perfection of Bauhaus skyscrapers.

But there is a dark side to our desire for order, a point where the glockenspiel becomes demonic. Located only thirty minutes away from Munich, among tidy farms and neat suburban houses, is Dachau. To enter the camp, which is now an international memorial to those who died under the Nazi terror, is an eerie experience, like being a tourist in Hell. Time seems to have healed little or nothing here.

It all looks so terribly familiar: low whitewashed buildings trimmed in gray; neatly raked gravel; not a twig, or a tree, or a flower. Ignore the barbed wire at the top of the fence, and it could be a factory or your high school, a laboratory or a state hospital. Dachau is so neat, so inhumanely neat, and it was just as neat forty years ago, kept clean at the cost of incredible suffering. Signs in the barracks inform us that prisoners who did not make their beds exactly four inches high were often executed; dropping a cigarette butt on the white gravel was a capital offense.

From the neatness of Dachau we learn once again that compassion and perfection do not exist well together. Love—as we all know but often forget—is often messy and unpredictable, disorderly as a young child's room. That we should expect mechanical reliability from machines is reasonable, but that we should expect it from one another is not only mistaken but terrifying in its consequences. Yet the more we interact with our computers, our answering machines, our television wristwatches, our stereo headphones, microwave ovens, automatic garage door openers, vibrators, cuisinarts, dustbusters, and programmable vacuum cleaners, the more likely it becomes that I will confuse them with you and you will confuse them with me.

Human beings—when compared to machines—are slow, imprecise, impatient, and incredibly creative. I am convinced that at its most fundamental level this creativity of ours is a form of erotic energy, yet I have found it increasingly difficult to define the erotic in any final way. Slowly I have come to realize that this is because erotic energy itself is protean, a living thing that takes many different forms, changing even while you attempt to examine it—sexual, of course, but more than sexual; spiritual but not religious—constant, perhaps, only in its mutability.

The art which emanates from this part of us must then be by nature ambiguous, disorderly, and incomplete, full of surprises, even at times confusing, marked by the prodigal variety of a jungle where a thousand different species of insects, plants, and mammals co-exist in a delicate, perpetually shifting balance. And for this reason I suspect that many people distrust it. They resent the fact that erotic art cannot be easily classified; it makes them uneasy, insecure, even hostile.

And this is totally understandable. Erotic art persists in violating our sense of decorum by perpetually reinventing itself. Sometimes it is beautiful, sometimes as gummy as wet clay, sometimes shallow, sometimes unexpectedly profound. We want it to hold still. We want an aesthetic of the erotic, a standard, so we can separate the poems, plays, novels, photos—the whole mess—into the pornographic and the socially significant, the sleazy and the sublime.

We begin to suspect that perhaps we've been duped, that we've been sticking pins in water. Why can't erotic art quit changing and let us examine it properly? But maybe if it ever quit changing it wouldn't be erotic art anymore; maybe it would be something else altogether.

A glockenspiel perhaps?

Colors

Festive Snow

Steven DaGama

San Salvador: juvenile guerrillas creep through
undergrowth. East and West Berlin: celebrants, weeping,
pickax their wall. Bucharest: a doomed autocrat

boasts his boulevard is wider than Champs Élysées.
He seals his borders. Prague: police batons fail to fracture
a multitude. Spirit prevails. Quebec: you kneel

astride me at your casement window and peck
the panes for a torchlight procession of ice skaters
booting festive snow. Mireille Mathieu sings

Pardonne-moi ce caprice d'enfant—I tilt you
against my chin, *chérie*, like a punch bowl of brandied cocoa.
You wrest off your crochet sweater, and sway.

Colors

Steven DaGama

Dakar woman (independent of the Senegalese
group touring Macao)—you brace yourself
against a stall, adjust coral red garters
through the slit of your indigo *cheongsam*.
Sight blurred to poetry but not to trinkets,
casual, lunch-drunk American couples bargain
and guffaw. Dakar woman—my clenched fists
unclenched would slip your frogs; my thumbs
would trace your collarbone on our veranda,
in our hammock. This green breeze unfurls us.

Learning How to Love

Richard C. Zimler

The phone rang at eleven in the morning last Saturday, and a man speaking Italian introduced himself as Giovanni Masso's grandnephew, Marco. He said that Giovanni had had a bout with bacterial pneumonia and was not expected to last much longer. If I wanted to see him alive again, I'd better get there fast. When I hung up, my thoughts were calm; numbness has always been my mind's first line of defense. I explained what the call was about to my wife, Angie. After that, I remember drinking black coffee and packing a bag very neatly, as if my shirts might break, but not much else. At Kennedy Airport, Angie told me that she'd finally reached our kids at college and told them we'd be away for a while. They'd both sent Giovanni their love. Our flight to Milan left at four in the afternoon, arrived at eight in the morning Italian time. On board, I smoked cigarettes and tried to read. At Da Vinci Airport, Angie and I caught a taxi to Milan's central station, then boarded a train for Turin. I sat close to her; she never wears perfume, and her warm scent has always made me feel protected. My hand rested on her thigh while I looked out the window. Marco was waiting at the end of the platform when we got off. He was lean and wily looking, had black hair gripped tightly into a ponytail. He said he recognized me from his great-uncle's photographs.

Marco's apartment was a showcase for leather and glass furniture. It had a view over the Po River and the faded mansions on its banks. It was June, and everything was very green. Giovanni was staying in the guest bedroom. When I saw him, it seemed as if I'd reached the end of a long slow race—the tortoise coming to the finish line. I took a deep breath and stared. He'd been packed like a mummy under a blue woolen blanket. He was asleep. Only his head and his right arm were visible. Pneumonia had given him a gaunt and vulturine face, and stubble bristled on his chin. He was so pale that he was gray—the color of cigar ash.

Only his hair was the same; it was still thick and white, had been mussed up into a great white crest. He heard our footsteps, awoke, and reached out a trembling hand. *"Chi è?"* he asked without opening his eyes. His voice was a hoarse whisper.

My heart was pounding out a panicked message about mortality, and I could not speak. My wife replied, "Alberto and Angela."

A smile pursed his lips, but his eyes remained closed. I walked to him, and he grasped my hand. I sat on a wooden chair that had been pulled next to the bed. Angie eased down next to him on the other side of the bed and began combing his hair with her hand.

"Thank you both for coming," he whispered in Italian. For a moment his lips moved like he was preparing to say more, but he did not speak. He fell back to sleep and breathed softly.

After a while, my wife and I looked at each other. We began to discuss the room decorations in hushed tones. It was one of those conversations people have when they're not at all prepared to have their hearts broken. We discussed the marble clock on the mantel, the Persian rug at the foot of the bed, the thin greenish light given off by the halogen lamp standing in the corner. I felt close to her, as if she were the only person in the world I could bear seeing. Then we fell silent and moved apart into separate thought. Giovanni awoke a short time later and said, *"Acqua."*

There was a glass of water on his night table. I lifted it to his lips. Water dribbled down his chin, and I wiped it with my sleeve. I took a sip myself. He said, "Alberto, I want you to read a story—'The Writer.' Ask Marco to get it for you." He patted my hand. "Read it because I want you to forgive me."

"Forgive you?"

He nodded and licked his lips again. His eyes opened for just a moment, as if to check that I was still there.

"Giovanni, I don't understand," I said.

In English, he replied, "Dear boy, you never understand

other people's bad intentions." Then he added in Italian, "It's one of your endearing qualities. Just read." Hearing him call me "dear boy" revived so many memories that I brought his hand to my lips and kissed it. I held his palm over my nose, let his fingertips touch my eyelids. I breathed in his scent. Giovanni's hands had always smelled of tobacco and soap. Now, they smelled of nothing. It frightened me.

As I placed his hand back down to the blanket, he said, "You'll see. It's just that I wanted so much for you . . ." His voice trailed off. "Just read it. Then come back tomorrow and we'll talk. I'll be stronger tomorrow."

He fell back into a kind of sleep, and his face solidified like a death mask. I only noticed then that on the wall above his pillow had been taped his beloved talisman. He'd shown it to me for the first time thirty-six years earlier. Sticklike figures were drawn on it—representations of his three protectors, the Jewish angels Sanoi, Sansanoi, and Samnaglof. The lines of their bodies were formed by minute Hebrew letters spelling out the first verse of Genesis.

After Angie had arranged Giovanni's blanket under his chin and smoothed its contours over his chest, we left the room.

When we'd seen him two years before, his face was full of color, and he had walked without difficulty. Despite his eighty-five years, he'd been witty and inquisitive. It was a terrible shock to now see him so fragile and silent, but I held my tears until I was in the hallway. Marco handed me some scented tissues. I blew my nose. He walked us into his study and gave me a brandy. I had a tremendous headache. Smoking only made it worse. Marco sat behind a glass desk and talked about Giovanni's stay in the hospital. My wife stood at the window and watched the river. She was chewing on the ends of her silver hair. When Marco fell silent, I told him that Giovanni had told me to get from him the short story *"Il Scrittore."*

"It's in his first collection," Marco replied. "You never read it?"

"No. I didn't really care for his early work. Too obscure. Like he was waiting for a club of French intellectuals. I much preferred his later things."

"You're the only one, then."

Angie whipped around and glared at Marco down the length of her nose. "Not the only one!" she said fiercely. She gripped her hair at the nape of her neck so that her round face ceased to be framed. Her cheeks were red, inflamed with anger. Her black Sicilian eyes bore down on him.

"I only meant the critics," Marco answered. He put a stick of gum in his mouth, then left the room. He came back a moment later with a thin paperback. "You both must be exhausted," he said as he handed it to me. "Take it with you to your hotel. We'll talk more in the morning."

Angie and I took a taxi to the Villa Pracci, a salmon-pink mansion high up in the hills across the river. Giovanni and I had stayed there when we visited Turin together in 1961 and '63. As we drove, Angie circled my thigh with her hand as if I were in danger of escaping. I leaned my head against the cool window, looked past tall cypress trees and tawny-colored tile rooftops at the central city below. The grid of Turin looked lovely. I cursed myself for not having visited Giovanni at Christmas.

Our room was on the top floor of the Villa. I'd chosen it because it had a vaulted ceiling that made me feel pampered. While Angie dozed off, I sat at the desk and started to read Giovanni's story.

The narrator is a young professor of literature at the University of Milan who is also a fiction writer. His name is Pietro, and he is an Italian Jew from a small town in Tuscany, Pitigliano. He comes from a poor family, is the son of a *shohet*, a kosher butcher. But he's very snobbish and although his first published novel recounts the history of an unhappy Jewish family, he does his best to play down his religious identity. It is ironic, then, that he receives an invitation from the Jewish community in Buenos Aires to travel there and give some readings. He agrees to go because he very much wants to see South America.

The story is written in the convoluted style which Giovanni employed in his early work and which won him such admiration from European critics.

While in Buenos Aires, Pietro enters a waterfront bar and encounters a young prostitute named Renata. She is small and slightly built, has great brown eyes rimmed with mascara, long black hair. She wears a tight red dress which descends to a ruffled fringe. She looks to the writer like a flamenco dancer. She speaks perfect Italian, explains that she comes from a family which has its origins in Genoa.

Pietro is ashamed of his simple Jewish past, of course, and he invents an aristocratic upbringing in a Catholic family from Florence. He says that the family patriarch, his father, makes ecclesiastical garments for the Church. Here, Giovanni's complexity of style beautifully emphasizes the intricate web of lies he spins. The sentences are as tangled as his story. The only true statement the writer makes is that he has led too cloistered a life to have ever slept with a prostitute. He asks why she has chosen such a profession. To his surprise, she replies, "Willingly and without shame." She explains that she became a prostitute to escape her father. He had begun raping her by the time she was twelve. Her tone is matter-of-fact as she describes his abuse, but the details are startling. There is an entire page of description of her father's hands in his different moods, how they bloated and hardened when he became drunk and began to attack her. Apparently, he used to penetrate her with his fingers before intercourse. They were cold. Dirt was crusted underneath his fingernails. He sometimes stuck them into her ass, made her feel like filth.

Even today, she says, his hands come to her in nightmares.

This honesty about sex is very uncharacteristic of Giovanni's early work. Until his whole approach to writing changed in the early 1960s, he was considered a stylistic innovator in Italy, but also something of a puritan.

Pietro ends up taking the prostitute back to his hotel, but they don't sleep together. They stay up all night talking. Renata traces her family lineage for the writer. She ends her narrative with the story of her great-great-great-grandfather, Don Giuseppe Cardinale, one of Garibaldi's lieutenants on his South American campaigns. He fell in battle during the Uruguayan civil war, she says. His head and both his arms are buried in an underground vault in the central church of Constitucíon; the rest of him was never found. Renata says that her father carries around Don Giuseppe's ring finger as if it were the relic of a saint. He wears it around his neck on a golden chain. Occasionally, she says, he would probe it inside her ass as he raped her.

After Renata's narrative ends, Pietro asks her what she could possibly believe in after having had such experiences. The Devil? An instinct for survival? She tells him that she believes only in food. At first, he despises this response as the product of a peasant mind. But then she goes on to explain a theory on the relationship between food and culture which he finds fascinating.

The dialogue from this section of the story is taken from a talk Giovanni and I had had in 1959 with a young woman from Buenos Aires named Anita. I didn't think anything unusual about this duplication, however; writers often re-use actual conversations in their fiction, of course.

The reader of Giovanni's story is set up to expect a sentimental ending. But the writer does not fall in love with Renata or pity her her fate. Instead, he tells her that she has sinned against all that is holy. As a final coup de grace, he tells her that she undoubtedly provoked her father into raping her. Why does he behave so cruelly? Because it is clear by the end of the narrative that she is a better storyteller than he is! He is simply jealous!

As I finished the story, it seemed to me that it had two morals: the first, that honesty weaves better tales than lies; the second, that a man who invents his life with falsehoods despises the simple freedom of the truth-giver. Maybe I was reading too much into it, but I also felt that Pietro's fabrication of a new past for himself was an admission that Giovanni's own hermetic style of writing was based on a need to veil his own insecurities.

Whatever the case, I had no idea what the story had to do with me forgiving him, or even what I was supposed to forgive him for.

My wife was soundly asleep by this time. I drew the curtains closed, crawled into bed, and spooned up behind her. It was three in the afternoon. I slept well but awoke at nine in the evening because my internal clock was so screwed up. It was dark. Turning on a lamp behind me, I read Giovanni's story again. I still didn't understand what the snobbish young writer's encounter in Buenos Aires had to do with me. When I paged forward to see if there were any acknowledgments or a dedication, I discovered that the date on the copyright page was 1956. That struck me as odd; Giovanni and I had had our conversation with Anita about food and culture in San Francisco in 1959. So how could he have recorded it in his mind and used it in a story published three years earlier? Unless the copyright date were wrong.

My wife awoke as I lay in bed thinking. She was famished, so we took a taxi into town and ate a late dinner at a self-service restaurant, then sat at an outdoor cafe which had chaises and deck chairs more appropriate to an English garden party. We sipped our tea and fended off mosquitoes. When she asked me what I thought of Giovanni's story, I made an elusive reply; I didn't want to discuss it until I'd understood what it had to do with me. Angie grew angry and silent. We looked off in different directions. At two in the morning, we took a taxi home and went to bed.

We awoke together at sunrise. As she brushed her hair back off her forehead, she asked me why I'd acted coldly toward her the night before. I replied that I was puzzled about the story and Giovanni's need for my forgiveness. I explained that my only clue was the conversation from 1959 which was apparently published in 1956. She said, "Tell me everything about your encounter with Anita. That must be the key."

I said, "You know the story. It'll just bore you."

She replied, "I know what you've told me. But I'm sure you've left things out. I'm not stupid."

I was silent for a while, so she said, "Look, we'll have breakfast sent up. Just begin at the beginning. And don't leave anything out. I know you fucked her more than once, so don't worry about hurting me. It was before we met. I don't care."

So I told her that it all began in July of 1958 when *A Land of Silence* was published. It was Giovanni's third novel and his first translation into English. The response was highly favorable. Edward Branting, writing in the *New York Times*, called him "a luminescent stylist and storyteller—the Milanese answer to James Joyce." Reviews in *Harper's* and the *Saturday Review* were also laudatory. The book was considered a success.

To cash in on all the hubbub about a "newly discovered" writer, Giovanni was scheduled to come to the United States in January of 1959 for a book tour sponsored by his American publisher, Simon and Schuster. A senior editor there, Robert Hutchinson, was an old friend of my father's. He asked if I would accompany Giovanni as his translator. I was fluent in Italian because my mother is from La Spézia, a small city on the Ligurian coast. We'd spent nearly three years there when I was eight, nine, and ten years old so that she could be with her dying mother and then help her father during his time of intense grieving.

Despite my language skills, I did not consider myself a logical choice as a traveling companion for Giovanni, and I was tempted to refuse. In the first place, I was only twenty-one years old. Giovanni, in 1959, was fifty-three. I imagined that I would be under the constant surveillance of a surrogate parent—an Italian parent to boot. Also, despite my bachelor's degree in Anthropology from the University of North Carolina, I was a functional illiterate. Mr. Hutchinson had told me that Giovanni was a sphinx, "half-man, half-encyclopedia." When he said that, I sensed that I would appear to be an even bigger idiot than I was in close proximity to this sphinx. In the end, however, I agreed; more than anything else except daily sex with any girl bearing even a slight resemblance to Monica Vitti, I wanted to travel. Since I was a hopelessly timid young man and considered a healthy sex life far beyond my means, I opted for second best.

I met Giovanni for the first time at the bar of the Waldorf-Astoria Hotel. Simon and Schuster had flown me up from North Carolina for his New York engagements. Right away, I spotted two hands spreading an issue of *Il Corriere della Sera* at a corner table. On his left ring finger were two wedding bands, one in silver and one in gold; at the time, Giovanni was still married to his wife, Lea. His right index finger bore a gold ring with a small pink stone—a cabochon tourmaline. His hands were thin but strong. Tufts of hair sprouted by his knuckles.

Giovanni must have spied me from afar or sensed my approach; he set down his paper as I walked toward him and stood up. He was tall and lean, had a shock of thick gray hair, clear blue eyes, a long straight nose. He wore a black suit, pink shirt, and thin blue tie. On the table in front of him were metal-rimmed spectacles, a glass half-filled with whiskey, a gold lighter, and a pack of Italian cigarettes—MS, I believe he was smoking then. All in all, I considered him distinguished but odd looking, something like my image of a brilliant philosopher. There was no doubt that he exuded an air of importance and self-control. I was frightened.

We shook hands stiffly. I spoke first, said, *"Buona sera, Dotore Masso. Sono Alberto."*

I thought it best to start out formal and work our way down

from there. I expected that he'd be impressed that I'd called him *"Dottore"*—at the time, everyone in Italy who had achieved a certain esteem was given this title regardless of any academic degrees he might or might not have been awarded.

He held up his index finger with the tourmaline ring and waved it back and forth at me. "Doctor, no," he said in English. "Giovanni, yes." He smiled so that I knew he meant well.

"Giovanni, yes," I replied, imitating his thick accent and earning a grin for my effort.

"Vorrebbe un whiskey?" he asked me.

I refused the drink because in those days I considered myself too young for hard liquor, then refused a cigarette for the same reason. We sat down, and he sighed theatrically. "You are incorruptible," he said. "But I cannot talk to you if you don't drink or smoke." He ordered me a dry red wine. "Even a virgin can drink red wine," he observed.

I was embarrassed that he thought me a virgin. True, I'd only had one, very awkward sexual experience with a hesitant young co-ed from Myrtle Beach, but I considered that experience definitive.

Giovanni looked me up and down as if he were assessing a young racehorse. I was growing more nervous, so I said, "Mr. Hutchinson told me that you're from Turin."

"Yes. I was born there and did my schooling there until I reached university age."

"I visited Turin a few times when I was little," I said. "My parents and I spent three years living in La Spézia."

He dangled a cigarette in his lips and leaned forward, intrigued. "What did you see in Turin when you visited?"

"All I really remember is the Egyptian Museum. It was the first time I'd seen mummies or hieroglyphics. And all that dust everywhere—it really did look ancient. I'd never seen so much dust in all my life. I was greatly impressed!"

He laughed. "Yes, they still don't clean the place very well. I never saw the dust in a positive light until now."

I said, "I think that going to the museum gave me the idea of studying other cultures for the first time."

Giovanni lit his cigarette and asked me what I meant. I explained about my degree in Anthropology, told him that I was actually most interested in studying European folk music. For that, I said, I'd have to go back and get a graduate degree in Ethnomusicology.

All this was true, but I made my plans sound more definite than they were because I was still smarting from being called a virgin and didn't want to be taken for an indecisive youth. He was overjoyed to discuss music, and went on to tell me about the different modes used in Italian folk chant. He discussed how in Sicily people still sang in the Arabic minor mode and how in Trieste melodies also took on the contours of Middle Eastern music because of the influence of Turkey. I didn't understand music theory, but Giovanni drew diagrams of scales and chords on napkins. That first night with me, he was inquisitive and warm, very enthusiastic. I began to study his movements and patterns. I learned, for instance, that he leaned forward whenever he wanted to make a difficult point or ask a question which might require a long response. He liked to have a cigarette lit when he started an explanation, and he squinted when he wished for me to say truthfully whether I'd understood. He had a lovely voice, deep and assured. His hands were always whirling and twisting. At times, it seemed as if he were trying to sculpt his thoughts. As a result of too much drink, he ended up complimenting my command of Italian and my intelligence with a string of exuberant adjectives. "We shall get along just fine," he concluded.

That first night we stayed up talking until one in the morning. I came away feeling distant from my own thoughts; I was still so young that it was impossible for me to imagine anyone over twenty-five years of age being my friend, let alone a famous writer of fifty-three. I didn't know how to define Giovanni's place in my life, went to bed feeling as if I'd stepped through a magician's hat into another world.

I once read that a three-dimensional object when entering a two-dimensional world could not appear as it really is. Imagine living on a sheet of paper, for instance, and that you can only see what crosses the plane of that paper. In that case, a sphere in three dimensions will look to you like a circle; a cube like a square.

That is what happened with me and Giovanni. I was unable to perceive him as he really was, so, over the next few days, he slowly took on the outlines of an avuncular college professor. Obviously, I chose an image familiar to me. And more importantly, perhaps, an image that was safe.

Giovanni and I met for breakfast each morning at 9 A.M. in order to review our plans for the day. On our third morning in New York, he said, "Today, Alberto, we're going to write to Mr. Branting before we do anything else."

I asked who he was, since I hadn't read Giovanni's novel, let alone Branting's review of it in the *New York Times*. He replied, "An unfortunate man who thinks I'm from Milan. And who believes that I write like James Joyce! We shall tell him that although I live at present in Milan, Turin is my true home. And we shall mention that comparisons are better saved for soccer players judging the size of one another's *cazzi* in locker rooms!"

Giovanni spoke with the outrage of any Italian whose regional affiliation has been mistaken or denigrated.

Back in his room, he dictated the letter in Italian while he sat on his bed and nibbled on the end of his glasses. Despite his indignation, his tone was dignified. For my translation, I took out some of the Continental formality which sounds ridiculous in English and softened some of his words; at the time, I thought that risking offending people was unnecessary. We never got a reply from Mr. Branting. It is worth noting, however, that his reviews of Giovanni's two subsequently published novels were scathing. "Such failure in one so generously gifted is a terrible thing to behold," was the cudgel he used both times.

In the first three cities of our tour, Boston, Toronto, and Philadelphia, Giovanni and I continued to get along famously. I began to discover the eccentricities to his personality. Like most Italians I have known, he was tremendously superstitious, for instance. He feared the evil eye and kept talismans. In particular, he valued the one which I saw over his bed in his grandnephew Marco's apartment. He explained its significance to me while we were eating dinner in Philadelphia: "I met a girl once named Mira who was the daughter of the rabbi of Pitigliano," he said. "It's a medieval village in Tuscany which the Jews call 'Little Jerusalem' because over ten percent of the population, perhaps 300 people, are Jewish. That's a very high percentage for Italy, you see. Mira was kind enough to take me to her home to meet her illustrious father, and hanging over the bed of her baby brother's cot was a talisman of three angels. Their names are Sanoi, Sansanoi, and Samnaglof. They protect infants and pregnant mothers from Lilith. So I had one made for me."

"Who's Lilith?" I asked.

"Originally, I believe, she was an Arabian night demoness. But the Jews transformed her into a Queen of *Sitra Ahra*, the Other Side. She lives to kill babies, strangles them. But my three angels can defeat her every time."

"Are you trying to tell me that you're a baby who needs protection from a Jewish demoness?" I inquired.

He replied very seriously: "My addition to this folklore, dear boy, is that Lilith sees all men as newborn babies. To her and to all entities from the Other Side, we all look alike. So I need protection from her and many other demons besides."

I must have shown my skepticism, because he said, "Soon, the shadow of other presences will enter the world which you and I have made together. Dear boy, remember, it takes time to see a man's real shadow. Wait and see!"

I had never heard anyone speak about himself as if he were dangerous, and I was fascinated.

It was in Chicago, just two days after this conversation, that this shadow of Giovanni's began to cover us both. We were in the habit of dining together every night, sometimes with local literati contacted by Simon and Schuster, sometimes alone. But that evening, after we'd finished a late afternoon autograph session at a bookstore on Michigan Avenue, he said, "I cannot be with you or anyone else tonight." His tone was cold, and he strode away from me as if I'd offended him. I canceled our dinner engagement for that night. He only returned to our hotel at three in the morning; we had adjoining rooms, and I heard him stumbling about. He broke either a lamp or a glass and shouted, *"Merda!"*

The next day, he accused me of mistranslating his speech to the members of Chicago's Italian-American Cultural Institute. "You're as dense as lead," he told me. "And you don't understand subtlety." He dismissed me with the wave of a lord displeased with a servant.

I was so stunned and humiliated that I cried when I got back to my room. I almost called my parents to tell them I needed money to fly home early, but there was only a week left to our tour. And my pride was at stake, of course.

After that, we spoke together only when necessary. The final insult came in St. Louis when he said that the reason Mr. Branting hadn't written a reply to him—care of Simon and Schuster, as we'd requested—was that I'd mistranslated his letter. He had proof, he said. When I asked him what his proof was, he told me he didn't wish to speak with a virgin who didn't drink or smoke.

From that point on, in New Orleans and Los Angeles, Giovanni refused to have dinner with me or any of the people contacted by his publisher. He spent his nights out alone and came back early in the morning. He began to get bags under his eyes, started drinking whiskey at breakfast. I reasoned that he was an alcoholic and decided that I should feel sorry for him. In truth, I hated him for making me feel incompetent and puny.

In San Francisco, Simon and Schuster put us up at the Mark Hopkins—as usual, in adjoining rooms. It was our last city on the tour, and I was greatly relieved. The City Club had sponsored a cocktail party at the Palace Hotel at six in the afternoon on the day we arrived. I stood next to Giovanni, provided translation for all the chatting. Despite too many whiskeys, he somehow managed to be clever and witty. By that time, I had begun to despise his Continental charm. I thought it was a mark of shallowness, if not a covering for a true Machiavellian evil.

When we had a moment alone, he put his arms over my shoulder and said to me, "Dear boy, there is someone coming to meet me tonight whom I think you will like. The niece of an old college friend. I've never met her, but she is supposed to be quite lovely. Her name is Anita." He took off his glasses. His blue eyes twinkled, and an amused expression twisted his lips. His tone, for the first time in a week, was friendly. I didn't know what to make of it.

About an hour later, a stunning young woman walked over to us at the cocktail party. She looked to be about twenty-five years old, was wearing tight jeans and a burgundy woolen sweater without a bra. She had firm, large breasts. Her nipples were pushing out on the fabric as if they wanted to be freed from confines.

When you're twenty-one and as horny as a rooster, you notice things like that even before you notice a girl's face.

But she was pretty as well, had dark and intelligent eyes, thick lips, long brown hair. She wore no makeup, which in those days was unusual. Mostly, I remember her eyebrows. They were thick and dark, and they joined together at the bridge of her nose. Years later, in an exhibition at the Brooklyn Museum, I saw these same eyebrows in a self-portrait by Frida Kahlo.

In the first few minutes of our conversation, I let Giovanni do all the talking. From a certain reticence in Anita's speech pattern and a look of warm solidarity for me in her eyes, I imagined that she preferred my silence to his charming conversation.

The Book

Giovanni asked her to dinner and made a show of inviting me along. He told Anita that I was the cleverest and most interesting American he'd met. That ridiculous assertion made me think that he wanted to play matchmaker. I reasoned that he thought an affair with Anita might make me a more interesting person. I wondered if perhaps he'd grown angry because I'd started to bore him. Maybe he was simply one of those people who needed to be entertained all the time.

Anita told me at the cocktail party that she was from Buenos Aires, the daughter of Italian immigrants from Verona. Six years earlier, her family had fled the Argentinean dictatorship because her father was a journalist and had received death threats. She was studying painting at the San Francisco Art Institute.

I'd never met anyone from South America before and was curious what it was like. As we walked to our restaurant, she explained the people of her city to us: "It's commonly believed that everyone in Buenos Aires is either a whore or a pimp. But that is not true. What is true is that most everyone there, with the possible exception of the Jews and Gypsies, *thinks* like a whore or pimp. The men wear pin-stripe zoot suits and gray felt hats and believe they own their woman. The women wear tight and colorful dresses that show off their contours and are proud to be owned by a well-dressed man. As for our government, everyone is on the take. Any official who does not accept bribery is considered stupid or a Jew. Or both."

"So do you think like a whore or pimp?" Giovanni asked.

Anita licked her lips as if savoring her reply. "A whore," she smiled. "But a renegade; I work for myself."

"Sooner or later, you may need a pimp for protection," he observed.

"Ah, that is one of the happy things I have discovered about North America," she replied. "I can sleep with a man here without need of protection. North Americans are less dramatic, less prone to destructive jealousy. You see, Argentines all wish to be stars of their own operatic productions. Americans simply want to star in their own television comedy."

I found her amusing and observant. I prayed that I had the courage to ask her straight out to sleep with me.

We ate dinner at a Chinese restaurant on Grant Street that was Anita's favorite. It was there that she explained her belief in a close connection between food and culture. The discussion we had was the same one which the Jewish-Italian writer and prostitute have in "The Writer."

Anita said that you could divide the regions of the world according to what kind of fat or oil the people in them used for cooking. Northern Europe, for instance, was a butter-based culture; southern Europe, from Provence on down, was olive oil–based. Brazil and much of sub-Sahara Africa cooked with palm oil, whereas many Middle Eastern peoples used the pouches of fat contained in a ewe's tail. At certain extremities on the globe, such as northern Canada, other animal fats were used—whale blubber, for instance. Now, according to Anita, these different oils affected personality. Butter eaters tended to be sexually puritanical, stolid, hardworking, and responsible. Olive oil people were more gregarious and sexually liberated, but decidedly unreliable. And so on. . . . This theory also had implications for ethnic conflict, she went on to explain. For instance, butter and olive oil eaters could coexist fairly well. Olive and ewe's tail people also tended to cohabit peacefully. But butter and ewe's fat eaters could never be expected to get along. Nor palm oil and butter people. She had drawn no particular conclusions about proper combinations for those who cooked with blubber. "Arctic people tend to stay put," she explained. "So we have very little evidence of what they mix well with."

I remember thinking that she might not just be lovely and intelligent, but also insane. Giovanni clearly enjoyed her talk, as well. "Dear girl, you are a joy to listen to!" he concluded.

As we were eating dessert, Anita reached over and placed

her hand on my thigh. I nearly jumped. Then she stepped her fingers to my zipper and undid it slowly and expertly. She felt her way inside my underwear. When I looked over at her, she was eating her tortoni as if nothing was happening. Very soon, of course, I had a throbbing erection. As she finished her dessert, Giovanni offered her a cigarette. She took her hand away from my sex to accept it. I tucked myself back in.

From this brief admission of interest on her part, I expected that I would be learning more about life that night, and that Giovanni might find me a more intriguing person in the morning. A dark pleasure pervaded me as I realized that, in some way, I'd be triumphing over him by winning Anita.

But that's not quite how it worked out, of course.

After the meal, as we stood outside the restaurant enjoying the cool night air, Giovanni asked Anita if she'd like to come back to our hotel and have a drink with him in his room. It was clear what he meant, and I realized that I was an idiot for even considering for a moment that he wanted to set me up with her. To my surprise and horror, she accepted his offer. When I looked at her, my face must have been full of adolescent yearning—of an accusation of betrayal, as well. She smiled mysteriously at me and hooked her arm in mine. Walking three abreast, we headed up Powell Street toward the Mark Hopkins. I noticed that Giovanni occasionally reached down to pat her behind as we walked. I cursed myself for being such an idiot. I begrudged him his experience and his ease with women.

In front of the door to his room, Giovanni bid me goodnight. Anita kissed my cheek. As she slipped into his room, she threw me an amused look over her shoulder and winked. The door closed. I stood in the hallway. I didn't understand.

When I entered my room, I could already hear the sound of kisses. Then there came a playful slap and audible moans from Anita. I took off my clothes, lay on my bed, and began playing with myself. I was desperate. I felt as if I would be justified in taking my own life.

Then, for a time, there was silence. I imagined that they were deeply submerged in lovemaking.

Suddenly, a knock sounded on the adjoining doorway between our rooms. Anita called my name. I ran to the bathroom for a towel and wrapped it tightly around myself to hide my erection. When I opened the door, I found her nude. Behind her, I could see Giovanni lying on his bed, also naked. He was smoking a cigarette and reading.

Anita pulled my towel away and dropped it to the floor. She came up to me, stood on her tiptoes, and kissed me. We embraced for a long time, and I pressed myself against her. She held my buttocks in her hands and licked her tongue across my nipples. Then she went behind me and lay against my back like a cape. I opened my eyes. Giovanni was standing by his bed, his erection pointing straight out. He came over to me. "Hello, dear boy," he said in English. He brushed his hand against my cheek and smiled sweetly, then leaned toward me. We kissed for a long time. When he dropped to his knees and took me in his mouth, I thought I would faint. I had never been so excited. I came almost immediately.

Anita, Giovanni, and I made love in his hotel room for two nights and three days. We missed all our appointments, explained to Simon and Schuster that Giovanni had come down with the flu. He hadn't our stamina and occasionally enjoyed watching Anita and I go at it. He'd caress our flanks and tweak our nipples as we explored each other—always with a very serious expression on his face. Once, he said to us, "There is nothing more lovely than watching two young people really fucking."

Occasionally, he read while we cavorted. Once, when I was inside Anita, he closed his book and started caressing my buttocks. I let him penetrate me from behind.

He is the only man I've ever slept with. I have no idea if I'm bisexual or was simply lucky to have met him. My fantasies are nearly always about women, but I was able to have great sex with him. How is this possible? I once asked him, and he replied, "We think people are more complicated than they are. You like sex. You like me. What could be simpler?"

I'm not so sure. I think that I enjoyed making love with him because nothing turns me on more than being desired. And my wife is the only other person who has ever desired me as much as Giovanni. That first night together, for instance, he lifted up his legs like a dog wanting its belly scratched and begged me to fuck him. Afterward, he made me promise to keep myself inside him while he fell asleep.

As we lay in bed the next morning, he explained why he'd gotten so angry with me on our tour. He confessed that he'd tried every way he knew how to seduce me, but that I'd been absolutely impervious to his efforts.

"You were trying to seduce me?" I asked.

"You see!" he said, knocking his fist against my forehead. "In matters of sex you are dense as lead ... impossibly stupid!" In his pitiful English, he said, "A screw be missing inside you head!"

He explained that the night he went out to dinner alone in Chicago he had reached his wits' end. He went out to pick up a man, but couldn't find anyone even mildly receptive to his advances. In St. Louis, the same thing happened. He began to suspect that it was through sorcery that I was preventing him from getting laid. He grew convinced that I was an asexual warlock. When Anita came to the cocktail party, he realized it was his last chance to get me into bed. He did his best to seduce her in order to get to me. Thankfully, she had a thing for older men. As they began to make love, he proposed a threesome. To his great relief, she'd eagerly accepted.

Those three days in San Francisco changed us forever. For my part, I realized that I could be sexually fulfilled and could fall passionately in love with a man. I started smoking, as well, a habit I've never been able to kick. I also learned that my professional calling had been staring me in the face practically all my life, and I decided to become a translator. It's a profession I've exercised these past thirty-five years, and I've no regrets.

As for Giovanni, when he went back to Italy, he separated from his wife. The need to hide his homosexuality dropped away along with the desire for obscurity in his writing. He adopted a more naturalistic and poetic style in his last six novels. Gay characters began appearing. None of them minced around, wrote melancholic poetry, or attempted a dramatic suicide. They were judges, artists, chefs, Mafia hit men, anarchist Fiat workers, retired Fascists. . . . One novel, *An Umbrian Autumn*, even featured an Italian-American translator from North Carolina. Italy in the sixties and seventies was hardly ready for such a wide-ranging image of gays. His books sold well in Rome and Milan, but his popularity elsewhere plummeted. He was even asked to resign his part-time job as a political columnist for *Il Corriere della Sera*. To his great credit, he refused, and the newspaper's management finally relented. The critics, however, thought he was perverse. "A great stylist has dried up and blown away," wrote a former close friend of his in Turin's largest newspaper, *La Stampa*, in 1961. That same year, another former friend wrote in *Il Messaggero*: "Mascherone today is no more than a male whore with a tiny pen." I know for a fact that this critic, Italo Gadda, was a closet queen who couldn't abide Giovanni's newfound freedom. In this case, jealousy provoked acidic vitriol—just as in "The Writer."

Yes, I am very bitter that a whole generation has grown up in Italy thinking him a marginal writer, and that all of Giovanni's books are out of print.

For a time I felt guilty about this turn in his fortunes, but he once told me: "I realized after I met you that it was love which had never before entered the tip of my pen. I could not have kept writing without letting it seek expression. I had no choice." Then he said something I'll never forget: "I realized that sex is a powerful truth—maybe the most powerful and ruthless truth of all. Because people's passions don't lie. Oh, they can be covered—hidden for an entire lifetime. But they don't lie. And if we dare to admit our passions, give them life, then they have the power to destroy every hypocrisy and mendacity in their path. So, in part, that's what I've been trying to do—create characters who allow their sex to speak."

After our time in San Francisco together, I never saw Anita again. When we left for New York, I took her address and phone number. The number turned out to be a Chinese hardware store on Stockton Street. The address didn't even exist. I figured that she'd enjoyed herself with us, but didn't want a repeat engagement.

Giovanni and I continued to sleep together during our last three days in New York, just before his return to Italy. I thought that I was gay, but it didn't bother me. When you're in love, those things don't seem to matter. Or maybe they still do matter to most people, but they didn't to me.

I waited two months while he resolved things with his wife, then moved in with him into a new studio apartment he bought in Milan. That was one of the most exciting time periods in my life; my range of emotion seemed limitless. Passion and terror and desire pounded in my chest, spewed from the tip of my cock, wedged themselves into my bowels. Through Giovanni, I also met some great people: Vittorio De Sica, Carlo Levi, Natalia Ginzburg, Tommaso Landolfi. We even ate dinner once at an outdoor cafe in Rome with my old heartthrob Monica Vitti.

Giovanni's longtime friends kept warning me what a selfish person he was, that I'd better watch out. But they knew another man. With me, he was tender, even doting. He was the most generous companion I've ever known.

In the end, however, we drifted apart. After about a year, he began to feel suffocated, grew alternately enraged and then morose. Sometimes, I think this happened because he was just waking up sexually after a long period of dormancy; he needed to sleep with other people and experiment. As for me, I realized that I wasn't uniquely oriented toward men after all. Our break-up was a nightmare for us both. When I arrived back in North Carolina, I felt as if I had been shipwrecked. Thankfully, Giovanni and I stayed friends and began to meet for lovemaking and conversation twice a year—once during the summer in Italy and once for Christmas in the United States. Then, in 1966, the sexual side of our relationship ended. Giovanni was in love with a Calabrian mailman named Claudio, and I'd fallen for a Sicilian-American weaver named Angela. We remained close over the next twenty-seven years, however. I always felt that our fates were bound together. As for Giovanni, I don't think that he could have loved me more had he given birth to me.

After I told all this to my wife, she said, "It's obvious why he wants your forgiveness."

"It is?"

She sat down next to me, held my hand. I was sitting up in bed. She said, "He seduced you. He thought he might have changed you sexually. Maybe he even thought that that's why we had problems in the beginning."

Angie and I had both had affairs during the first years of our marriage. For a time, we'd split up. "That's absurd," I said.

"A dying man thinks absurd thoughts," she replied. "He needs your reassurance."

I figured she was right and kissed her shoulder. "I appreciate you listening to all this. It can't be easy."

Angie turned away as if considering her feelings, then looked back at me and reached under the covers. She started caressing my balls and said, "What you did thirty years ago with your cock doesn't bother me. It's what you do with it now that counts."

"I don't know if I can," I said, but I was already growing excited. And I realized that despite what she'd said, she needed my reassurance as well.

She threw off the covers, took me in her mouth. When I closed my eyes, I pictured Giovanni kneeling before me. A pang of guilt for this mental betrayal made my erection suddenly wither back to nothing.

Giovanni used to tell me, "When you have a man's cock in your mouth, you can often tell what he's thinking." Maybe he was right, because Angie said, "Go ahead and fantasize about him if you like. Then come back to me."

Her words seemed to break a spell, and I pulled her up on top of me. When we got her jeans off, I entered her. We made love pressed to each other, as if we needed the friction of our bodies to keep the chill of winter away.

When we arrived at Marco's apartment that morning, we found that Giovanni's condition had improved, just as he'd predicted. He lifted one eye open in a humorous manner when we entered.

"Got a cigarette?" he asked me. His voice was still dry and hoarse.

"I'm sure you shouldn't smoke," I said.

"Shut up. I just want to put it in my mouth. Unless . . . if dear Angela doesn't mind, you prefer placing something else a little more poetic in there." He opened his mouth wide.

Somewhere along the line, Giovanni had decided that there was nothing more poetic than an erect penis. We laughed with the relief of those who believe that a loved one is going to recover.

I gave him a cigarette, and he kept it in the corner of his mouth.

"Did you read the story?" he asked eagerly. He sat up.

"Yes, but I'm . . ."

"And do you forgive me?"

"I don't understand what I'm to forgive you for. Do you really . . ."

"For hiring Anita," he interrupted aggressively.

I glanced over at Angie. She shrugged as if to say, "Don't look at me."

"Hiring Anita?" I asked.

"Still naive, eh? I paid her flight up from Los Angeles and gave her a hundred dollars. She was an aspiring actress, was hoping to become the next Gina Lolabrigida, poor girl. I knew about her through De Sica. He'd used her once in a film. Her real name was Carla, I believe."

"Why'd you pay her?" I asked.

"You're really stupid sometimes," he said, and he shouted, "I had to seduce you!" He had a coughing fit after that. When he was breathing calmly again, he put his cigarette back in his mouth and said, "I'd written her part the night before. Based some of it on a conversation I'd had several years earlier in Buenos Aires. Didn't you recognize the words?"

"Of course. But I thought that . . ."

"I couldn't take the chance of failing," he interrupted. "She studied her lines well, did a good job, don't you think? You found her fascinating. All that malarkey about Buenos Aires and butter and ewe's tails was just right for you." He rolled his eyes, looked at Angie and said, "You should have been there. It was a perfect setup." He looked back at me. "You wanted her badly, didn't you? And when she started making those noises in my room, those moans . . ." He lifted his eyebrows like a rogue.

"I hated you and her both," I said.

His face grew serious. "Come closer to me," he said.

I sat down next to him, and we held hands. "Do you forgive me?" he asked.

I leaned over, took his cigarette from his mouth and kissed him on the lips. For a time, we looked at each other as people do who aren't ready to say goodbye. Then I said, "There's nothing to forgive. You taught me how to love."

⟿

The Book

The next morning, just as I was shaving, we got a call at our hotel from Marco: Giovanni was dead. He simply never woke up. He didn't cry out in pain, had died peacefully.

Angie knew from my face what had happened and started to cry.

Marco told me that Giovanni had left me certain things in his will—two unfinished manuscripts, the tourmaline ring I'd always admired, his talisman of the Jewish angels. When I was up to it, I could come to his flat to collect them. Then he said that Giovanni had also left me his studio apartment in Milan. Marco added that he hoped that I would consider letting the family keep it instead. His tone was threatening. I was so shocked that I was unable to reply. I held out the phone to Angie. She took it and thanked him for his call.

The news of Giovanni's death left me inconsolable. I sobbed on and off all morning. Angie curled up behind me in bed and held me. Then, that afternoon, I wanted to walk in the streets and feel the comfort of people around me, of life. I was feeling desperately fragile, as if I might simply fall to the sidewalk and sit there crying like a child. Angie and I held hands and went to Giovanni's favorite restaurant in the city. It's a family place on the Rua Magenta that serves the most wonderful gnocchi in pesto sauce. Then we walked down the Via Roma toward the castle. It was sunny and hot. Suddenly, I felt a pang in my chest; I simply had to get to the Egyptian Museum. There, I admired all the dust on all those statues of animal-headed Gods. I remembered what it was like to be eight years old and to be discovering the world. It only made me sadder. But perhaps I needed to hug that sadness to me as hard as I could before I could leave for home.

Giovanni is the first person to whom I've made love who has died. It's a very strange feeling. It's as if a part of my sexual life, my heart, has been carried off to an underworld. I don't know what to make of it. I can feel his body against mine as if it were yesterday, remember how we made love that first time: his gray chest hairs rubbing against my smooth skin; his strong hands pressing into my shoulders; the taste of tobacco and wine in his mouth.

I do not want this taste to end, and I do not want him to be dead. I want him to be as handsome as he was when I first met him, to have him call me "dear boy." But mostly, I want to be learning how to love all over again.

This Close

Dorianne Laux

In the room where we lie, light
stains the drawn shades yellow.
We sweat and pull at each other, climb
with our fingers the slippery ladders of rib.
Wherever our bodies touch, the flesh
comes alive. Heat and need, like invisible
animals gnaw at my breasts, the soft
insides of your thighs. What I want
I simply reach out and take, no delicacy now,
the dark human bread I eat handful by greedy
handful. Eyes, fingers, mouths, sweet
leeches of desire. Crazy woman, her brain
full of bees, see how her palms curl
into fists and beat the pillow senseless.
And when my body finally gives in to it,
then pulls itself away, salt-laced
and arched with its final ache, I am
so grateful, I would give you anything, anything.
If I loved you, being this close would kill me.

For My Daughter Who Loves Animals

Dorianne Laux

Once a week, whether the money is there
or not, I write a check for her lessons.
But today, as I waited in the car for her
to finish her chores, after she had wrapped
this one's delicate legs, brushed burrs
and caked mud from that one's tail,
I saw her stop and offer her body
to a horse's itchy head. One arm up,
she gave him the whole length of her side.
And he knew the gesture, understood
the gift, stepped in close on oiled hooves
and pressed his head to her ribcage.
From hip to armpit he raked her body until,
to keep from falling, she leaned into him
full weight, her foot braced
against a tack post for balance.
Before horses, it was snakes, coiled
around her arm like African bracelets.
And before that, stray dogs, cats
of every color, even the misfits,
the abandoned and abused.
It took me so long to learn how to love,
how to give myself up and over to another.
Now I see how she has always loved them all,
snails and spiders, from the very beginning,
without fear or shame, saw even
the least of them, ants, gnats, heard
and answered even the slightest of their calls.

$\mathscr{B}$y Scent

Theresa
Vinciguerra

This moment we make love I see my own death,
feel it, palpable as the thick folds of drape
that hang close to our bed, over the sliding glass
door now slightly ajar for summer, for the slow-
motion breeze lifting the wide linen hem
into a delicate evening arch that hollows out,
seamless, by the corner of our sheets. I know
it is through one such tunnel, tenuous as this
I will disappear, become
untouchable.

Together we catch our breath,
hear the pulse, our hearts, stumble down
into the stillness after passion. Like the darkest
blood-red, in the rose veined blackest with tributaries,
we have given the fullest fragrance, have turned
our flowered parts inside out for love, while,
already in the shrinking fornices, decay spreads
its sweetness. Before the long hours of sleep
I rise to cleanse the blind perfumed crevice
that has led you into my body. How like petal flesh
unfolding, you said it was—making of me the garden
on the other side of the glass—a bed invisible
in the night, untravelled, except by scent,
by the sense that maps our inexorable way
to the very caves and roots that open
out into the dark.

he Rain

Nick Bozanic

Falling so absentmindedly on the morning
glories, the vines of summer squash,
the violet buds of nodding aubergines,
the rain might be dreaming of other gardens,
other days, other lovers
                        hurrying along
a brick-paved path past the crepe myrtle
blossoming like clouds of a sunset forecasting
fairer weather to the live oak's umbrella
of boughs, where they laugh and brush away
with their fingertips the beads of water
from one another's lips and brows;

and wandering off toward the lake (a slow
and halting progress, like one who goes
about a routine task distractedly), the rain
must be imagining that web of light
in the woman's hair, as the sun,
in the shower's wake, touches her there,
the pattern of gold and gray the shade
lays upon her face, making of it a mask
of Artemis,
            and how the man, alarmed by wonder
at the wilder beauty of her beauty transformed
by this trick of light and leaves, pauses—
so near her now he can taste her breath
between them—at the border of that other world,
where the delirium of desire delivers the heart
from dread;
            and she, as a cloud crosses the sun,

eclipsing his face with a shadow so deep he
seems a revenant, opaque and insubstantial,
closes her eyes to shut out the fear she feels,
abandoning her life to this.
                              They kiss.
And the rain in its reverie everywhere
erodes the reasonable present to reveal
the realms of passion forging upward
from below, as below the earth's
obdurate husk of dust and stone,
volcanic fires storm.

Baja

Donald
Rawley

You on the beach with a thousand birds.

They fly around us like guitar strings
and the sound of their breaking
when played hard into night.

My feet are smaller than yours
and burn in the sand.
I touch your oil
in this reserved light.

Take a swim, find water
petaled like a virgin's skin.
I shall discover my heart
purple as Africa
yellow as goldmine mud.

Have you felt the curled fur of Cirios
baking on the road to Catavina?
Or smelled the gasoline in Ensenada
and the fishermen's bars?

I'll put it on a plate for you.
I'll drink it straight up.

Just let me stay green in this sun
of unnamed rivers sided by moss.
Keep me green as a kid
off the bus in an open field.

And in dusks of tinseled slow mariachis
our roots suffocate.
Our breath twists up the hill
in flowers that sing.

We alone will hold in cliffs
of ocean, ferns and adobe.
Our arms will scrape meadows

sown with sunflowers
aching in rocky earth.

This is a heat of gardenias
bought in drugstores
left on nightclub tables
and brought home to teenage girls.

You don't see the parrots
walking rooftops in San Quentin.
They are wild and my age.
They are gargoyles mating
lime green and ferocious
as your grip.

It is within your mesqual vision
I want to reside numb
on a fresh hotel bed
like a cream mint
under a starched pillow.

I hear the hunting guns
off the Bahia Falsa.
The black brant fall
and will be strung in the street
then cooked with lard and beer.

I want to taste what your eyes
will see languid and caught.
You watch my moves
evaporate into Pacific wind.

I should be your guide
and tell you who I am.

Our skin has become sand.
It is fired terra cotta

to the boulders of El Pedregoso
and starched cholla jungles of Vizcaino.

We're naked in a desert
used to bones and water.
You drive faster until
the heat becomes a tunnel,
a liquid cloud behind us.

You were born to sire boys
daily in unknown villages
under a sun burning
the balls of your feet.

You could make me blind.
You could cast me into histories
and fraudulent heavens
disguised as Baja sky.

It's the bitter absinthe of your eyes
the stick of your hands.
It is how my addictions are added
by the tremors in your chest.

Tonight I want all that is sweet and kills.
Like sugarcane and trucked bananas
I want to steal cuts of you
to taste on deadened mornings.

San Ignacio jumps from a hollow
and makes us wet under palms.
It is an intoxication of leaves
cardon and mud
men bathing in dirty ponds
near hotels perfumed
with marijuana and pork.

You ask for mesqual with the worm.
Your face is mission stone.
It is painted wood
reserved for altars.

Here I see mountaintops
and seasons crying
as you close my eyes and plunge.

Iguanas stare at us in Mulege.
Here there is no allowance
for movement faster
than the flies who taunt their tongues.

This is scorpion weather
where we watch our feet.
Cirrus clouds erase
the chalk of an acidulous sun.

Here the queens of Spain
return as Mulege babies
cribbed on windowsills,
by fate Infantas plotting
from a lifetime of missing men.

The Cowboy Sestinas

Karen Lee Hones

Beginning

I get on the Greyhound in Reno at midnight,
survey the crowded bus, see that I have to wake up the man
in the second row, folded over with his hands
between his knees, his feet tucked in, his bald head
on the seat. He starts when I touch him,
sits up like a shot, turns on the light and pretends to read

Trinity. I take *Emma* out of my duffel, intending to read,
too, but hold it in my lap, absorbing the bus, the dark, the night,
the man next to me. I squirm, trying to get comfortable,
   nudge him
accidentally, apologize, and he says "That's all right, ma'am,"
introduces himself, adds, "You can put your head
on my shoulder if you want," turns off the light.
   I notice his hands,

medium size, muscular, callused and nicked, a worker's hands.
We sleep, the restless sleep of travelers. I wake up and read
the schedule to orient myself. We're in Winnemucca. His head's
on my shoulder, I shake him, rouse him from his night's
rest for breakfast. A manly wedge of a man,
Garrett, with big shoulders and slim hips. I follow him

to the Casino. He treats to coffee and toast. I warm to him,
a real cowboy with plaid shirt, boots, rough hands.
He pulls out a picture of his boys, Abe and Joe. A man
who loves his kids. One dark and one fair. Abe likes to read,
Joe likes to wrestle. Garrett says *rassel.* Tonight
he will reach his destination, Cheyenne. He puts his hat
   on his head

and we get back on the bus. I take a cat nap; my head
flops uneasily onto him. My body is accommodated by his
body. At the break we sit in the Interlude in Evanston
    sipping tallboys. Night
falls outside of Laramie and he turns sudden and sure
    and runs his hands
up and down my thighs and kisses me, I feel red
heat between us as my desire rises for this man,

oblivious to fellow passengers, wanton woman
I am, locked into it, my knee between his; he's hard
against me. Kitty corner from us an old lady turns on the light
    and starts to read;
we untangle ourselves. He wants me to get off with him
in Cheyenne. I'm on my way to a family reunion
    but can't keep my hands
off him. We have to get off while they service the bus;
    it's 9 at night—

Standing with a man in a dark corner of the station,
holding his hands, our heads leaning into a red brick wall,
I promise to spend the night with him some day.

Middle

The minute I get off the bus he says he wants to eat me,
presses his thumb to the place on my jeans
    where he will put his tongue,
The five minutes it takes to get to his ranch, I am
    smiling out the window
at the rain. We lie down in front of the fire and
    he pulls my jeans off,
spreads my thighs gently with his rough hands, touches my lips
with his fingers, licks me. He raises up, shakes his head and says,

"Mmmmm." I come right away, I was wet on the bus. He says,
"You taste so rich I feel dizzy." He peels off his clothes,
    warming me

with his hands. I am dripping, still. He kisses me, tastes my lips,
leaving my own flavor in my mouth, an acquired taste like garlic.
　　I'm tonguing
him as he reaches under my cheeks, separates them,
　　wipes some come off
and enters me. I am riding him when I see a face at the window,

a boy's flushed face. "Garrett, is that your son at the window?"
I whisper, sliding away from him. His eyes follow mine
　　and he says,
"Oh—Joe," with a glazed look in his eyes, pulling out and off.
He jumps up and starts pulling on his pants, shielding me.
I rummage around for my underwear,
　　and have to bite my tongue
to keep from laughing. The boy, Joe, comes in.
　　He has his father's molded lips,

but his own fair beauty. He is nervous, chewing on his lower lip,
doesn't know how to act. While I struggle with my clothes,
　　he goes to the window,
looks out at the rain. Garrett acts serious,
　　I am afraid Joe will be tongue
tied with us. But Garrett saves the day. He goes over to Joe
　　and says,
"Let's go get some Italian food." He looks over to see
　　I have made my
self presentable and puckers his mouth. We all go out
　　and take off

in his pickup truck. Joe sits in the middle. I feel like
　　I'm falling off
the seat, dazed from sex and discovery. My lips
are numb, full and helpless like at the dentist. Joe glances at me,
smiles. We get to the restaurant, seated at a table by the window,
order an extra-large pizza with everything. I say
"Usually I'm a vegetarian but when in Rome. . . ."
　　Garrett orders tongue

as an appetizer and I watch him eat it, chewing the tongue
with such pleasure. He has nice teeth. Joe is awfully
quiet and big-eyed but I think he likes me. I say
"I hear you like to wrestle," and he says yes, licking his lips.
After we eat the pizza, we go home, rain beating
    against the window,
insistent. Garrett reaches across Joe, touches me.

We play Clue, listen to country. At ten Joe, heavy-eyed,
    goes off to bed.
Garrett says where were we, goes to the window,
    pulls the curtain shut,
comes over to me, begins again with lips, tongue.

End

A second spring. What we have seems natural,
    so I call it friendship.
I don't mind the four-hour trip on the bus, getting up in the bleak
dawn to stand by the woodburning stove, watching him
    go out back
to slop the hogs. Often in the morning he says
    he just wants to "soak"
it, sore from the night but still hungry.
    On a particularly enchanting spring
day, I help him put rubber bands on the kids' balls. At the end

of a few days, they fall off.* On one part of his property
    a road dead ends
at a field where I lie with a novel in the tall grass
    while my friend
hacks away at the heavy overgrowth he has to cut down
    every spring.
The ground is damp, I am surrounded by sheep, even one black

* Rubber bands are placed around the testicles of young goats to remove them
eventually, thus preventing them from becoming "billy goats."

one. Garrett clears his land and I labor over my book.
   At night I soak
in the clawfoot tub, he tramps in in his boots, bends
   to scrub my back,

suck my nipples. Sometimes after dinner we take a
   coarse blanket back
out to the field, the odor of earth, sheep, and goats blending
with our juices. Thank God he's fixed. City mouse into
   country mouse, I soak
up the fullness of nature, carefree. This is an unusual friendship,
man, woman, connection without tension. He touches my black
hair, "so soft," drives me up to Mount Shasta, identifying spring

flowers along the road. Soon I return to the city, it's spring
there, too. On the track I run into a man who has been
   on my back
burner for years. He has a tight body in gray shorts.
   He has black
moods. The sap is still running from my days in the country
   and we end
up in bed. We burn for a month, I forget what it was like
   with a friend
who was safe. I try to let my feet touch the ground once or
   twice for the sake

of sanity, but proceed to surrender to passion, to try to soak
it all up. When Garrett calls, I am remote, feeding
   my new spring
fever. The night of the full moon I go see Van Morrison
   with a friend;

at 1:30 in the morning the lover comes over, begins
   to rub my back
and I turn to him. Van, the man, the moon. I am so
   turned on I end
up pregnant. That is the beginning of a black

period. When the lover challenges "me or the baby"
  I give him a black
look. I call Garrett, confide in him while soaking
in a hot tub. He is kicking himself for letting me go,
  letting me end
up back in the city, in trouble. He urges me to come up,
  stay through the spring,
but I am beginning to train for a new life, will never go back
again. He says he'll always be there when I need a friend.

One day the next spring the baby is soaking in her bath
  when the bell rings.
At the end of that day I am back in bed with Garrett,
  his rough hands
familiar under black pleated silk. Soon I will pass him to
  my best friend.

Little Fires

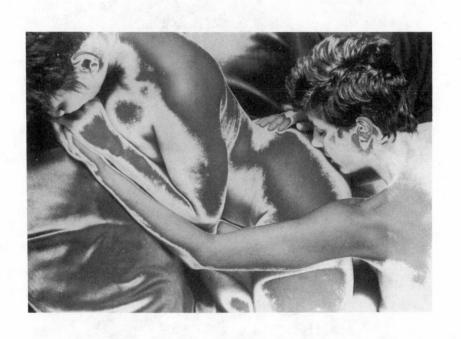

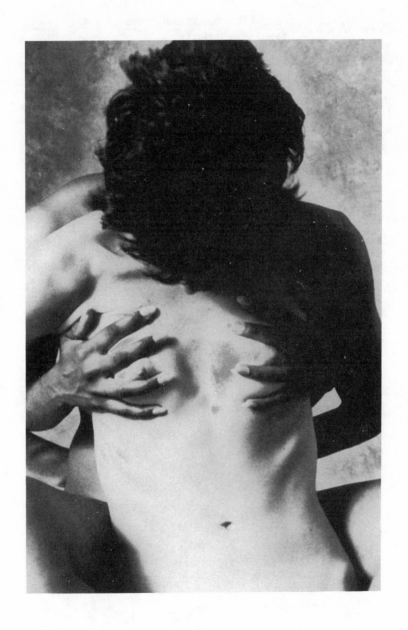

R-

David Mamet

White flowers dark
Thick eyebrows are a sign
Of great sexual health.
A walk in Westminster
A visage
Which evaporates upon examination.

Vast expanses
Of her soft, flat belly
Her smell on my face
Well. I will push my hands up
Underneath her vest.
No, not now. Later, though,
Right at this instant
Pushing through I saw:
God-sent entitlement,
Long, long adventures,
Sweet friends,
Vagrant hours beyond intensity
Love like a flower falling.

The American Woman in the Chinese Hat

⌐

Carole Maso

Everyone here is kissing everyone on the cheeks—twice, three times, four times this summer, one of the hottest in years I'm told on La Côte d'Azur, where I have come to write. But I'm not kissing anyone; I'm waiting for her.

She has written to me: "How much I miss you! Beneath all I do is an undercurrent of sadness at your absence. I think of you without knowing I am thinking of you, until I spring into consciousness and you are before me as clearly as the road I am driving or the fork I raise to my mouth—that close, that immediate, I love you so."

And I have written to her: "Come here and I will make you lamb with anchovy butter. Courgettes and Tomatoes Provencal Soupe de Poissons. I will wrap you in French cottons. I will bathe you in perfumes made from flowers not far from here."

I have come to Vence, a small resort town, ten kilometers from the sea, between Nice and Antibes, and I am sitting at the bar called La Regence.

La Regence. Everyone here is sitting under white umbrellas, drinking their drinks, tossing their heads, talking about *le cinema* or *la poesie*, or the great thinkers of France, in this beautiful place ten kilometers from the sea.

It had been a moody June, a month of cold and rain and wind, but now the luck has changed and everyone is out in full force to celebrate, to talk, talk, talk, to flirt, to languish in heat and light and I am caught in it all, in a whirl of polka dots and lace, in high heels and perfectly shaped legs, of light and stripes and sunglasses. Oh la la! At every table, *salut! Ca va!*

Waiters and waitresses glide by with trays of many colored drinks. The drink that is grenadine and beer, an intense rouge, the bright green drinks of menthe and the yellow *citron presse*. The cloudy drink that is Pastis. And *vin rose. Les glaces* fly by.

Marvelous ice cream concoctions arrive at the marbled tables topped with tiny umbrellas or fan-shaped cookies like wings.

Vacationers pose for photos: the small adored dogs on every arm. "Tootsie, *viens!*"

Children run around a circular stone fountain. Old men race by on *mobilettes*. People pass carrying *gateaux* and extravagant bunches of flowers. And on the street the large, expensive cars of summer drive by slowly for all to admire.

The young are engaged at every table in animated, intellectual conversation. *"Mais oui! Mais non! Mais bien sur! Voila!"* They fling around cigarettes and run their hands through their red tinted hair. During the lull they look around. They are not afraid to stare. I feel their eyes on my exposed back, on my shoulder, my leg. My foreign face.

"Ca va?" they say. *"Ca va bien,* and *à demain."* I love the way their voices rise at the end of their sentences, the way they sing their language.

She has written to me: "I was so sad there was no letter from you today. I wait every day for the letters to unfold, the French stamps, the pink paper. If only I could open one of your letters, put my lips against it and taste you. I must tell you my dove that I feel somewhat lost without you."

Pink drinks, sea-green drinks float by. And on the radio Sade sings about Paradise. Children in designer French clothes dart in and out of the palms. "Francois, *viens!*" A gloriously sculpted head goes by. All kinds of hats. It's the kind of light that makes you feel like you're seeing things for the first time.

"One feels safe from grief here," I write in my notebook.

I am known as the American woman in the Chinese hat who writes.

A girl passes who reminds me of her ten years ago. She must have Basque blood I think.

I close my eyes and picture her here, sitting under a white umbrella at La Regence.

In three months she will leave her job in finance and come

here to live. We will stay in a stone house with a red tile roof. We will live on olive oil and tomatoes, bread and figs, a few small fish. We will drink rosé from Bandol, white wine from Cassis, Cotes du Rhone. I will finish my book and she will do for the first time whatever she wants. Learn French. Learn to love this place as I have come to love it.

And I have written to her: "The dollar today is worth six francs and suddenly, mysteriously, magically I am richer. I'm sure you could explain all this to me—but here alone, going to the bank, it feels like another small miracle in a place of miracles."

La Regence. The plane trees cast an incredible shade. The young move in and out of light, singing American songs, Michael Jackson, Taylor Dayne, stars, this glorious day, in their own lives. I order another drink.

And I write to her, "I wish I could send you a hazelnut torte or a tarte citron. I wish I could send you the way the light falls on the baskets of women in town, or make a gift of the sound of bells on a Sunday."

I tremble when I hear a bit of Spanish, the language she still speaks in her sleep. Or when I see a cat that reminds me of our cat. To touch a cat. She will bring the cat, of course. And the absentee ballots.

And she writes: "Today Jay caught a sixteen-inch trout, that's almost twice the length of this paper, twice my poor trout that we ate on the porch dreaming of Antibes, dreaming of Tuscany."

I miss her so much. I am acutely lonely here without her. I am the American woman, *toute seule*, in the Chinese hat who writes. But it will not be long now. It's our last separation. It seems inconceivable to be apart anymore. I don't know why it's taken me so many years, but now I am finally certain. Now I know we're meant to be together. Life without her does not seem like real life. I see it with the clarity only this kind of light makes possible. The two of us together, forever. I have given up too much I think to write the two books I have written. I have given up too much to be the person capable of writing them. I have almost lost her as a result.

I write to her: "You are my dove. My *colombe d'or*."

And she writes to me: "I am going to plant the small plants we bought." She is going to make an herb garden. She is going to grow her hair.

I am trying to improve my French before she comes. *Venir* is to come. *Choisir* is to choose. *Besoin* is to need. *Attendre* is to wait.

They call the cats *mignon* here—little and sweet and dear, all in one word.

"*Tiens!*"

And she writes to me: "Be careful when the mistral comes. You know how absent you can be. You know sometimes you slam into every tree. Be careful. Remember how easily you bruise."

They call the children "*les petits*" here. Everywhere there are French babies. Little Francois has wandered away from his family again, this time to pet a white bird. "Francois, *viens!*"

I order another drink. I stare back at the young French man when he stares at me, and I hold my notebook for courage because so much courage is required. How the day dissolves in *salut* and *ca va*. How the day dissolves in Pastis. My eyes rest on a girl who has seated herself next to the young man who stares. She laughs with the carefree joie de vivre of a pretty young girl in early summer. She calls out to a friend passing through the square, "Pascal, *attends!*"

Attendre is to wait.

Another man comes up to me. I steer clear of desire. It's a choice I'm learning can be made. His eyes graze my leg. I want only her now. Still I write in my notebook, "One does whatever one must. One walks through fire if necessary, through light. Attracted to it like moths. One swims in treacherous waters like poor trout, *brochette*. Attracted to it like salmon to their deaths."

I'm drifting off. These strange hours of writing in the cafés and bars of Vence.

There is so much longing in me.

A fish, a woman, a vulture appears before my eyes. I can't stop from seeing this. A spear. Goats gambol around a dancing nymph. Fishermen devour their catch of sea urchins in darkness. I think of the great Picasso, who has given me this, painting in Antibes. It is 1946 and he has just met the beautiful Marie-Therese in the Galeries Lafayette and they are lying on the beach at Juan-les-Pins and they are about to go for a swim.

Something here is slightly dangerous. These strange hours of writing. Sometimes there's vertigo. Sometimes I lose the way home.

Love is what is dangerous under this bright surface of *saluts* and kisses and ice cream and many colored drinks in the dazzling afternoon.

I look up. Love should be like this: a blond boy in a striped shirt tipped back in his chair framed by bamboos and palms and large cars, eating a sandwich *jambon*. Only his eyes on my leg. Love should be like this. But it is not. Love is too imperfect, too hard. I think of our ten years together. I'm losing my concentration. I close my notebook. On the cover of a magazine at the next table it says, *"SIDA: les chats aussi."* I think of my friend Thomas, two years dead. He would have been thirty-four this month. He would have liked it here. One must take care in a foreign country. Without language there is no preparation, without familiarity things pop into your vision seemingly out of nowhere. Without warning, magazines like this one. "AIDS," it says, "cats too." I bruise so easily. One must take great care.

From this perch I can watch all the Vence regulars come and go. Names I would hope to someday know.

I am the American woman in the Chinese hat who writes.

Vouloir is to want.

Attendre is to wait.

I miss her.

How beautiful she would look in white under a white umbrella at La Regence.

I might make her a hat from a paper napkin.

We might order an ice cream with wings.

We might practice our French.

We might tear off the ends of a baguette.

We might drink Veuve Cliquot in our black dresses and try to guess the nationalities of all the people around us.

We might even allow the mistral to make us crazy; safe with each other.

Everyone is kissing everyone else. My favorite waitress is at the next table taking an order. She is wearing her day-glow clothes, her butterfly belt, her necklace of plastic leaves and fish and spears. The bus pulls up from Nice. A man steps off, comes up from behind, and caresses her. She turns. She is wearing her signature midriff top and she is in love.

Dimanche and the bells arrange themselves around the pure desire to believe. Each village rings out. Vence, St. Jeannet, St. Paul, Tourettes. I look into the faces of the faithful as we enter the ancient cathedral.

Marie, Reine de France. Inside, I memorize her flaring back, her steady gaze. *Elle est vierge toute pure. Elle est mère parfaite. Elle est reine du ciel et de la terre.* Mary, our Lady of Sorrows. I ask her for peace here. I ask her for patience and courage—because so much is required. I allow the mass to wash over me in French. *Ciel* is both the word for heaven and for sky, I think. I pick words out: *Toujours. Sans doute. Sans exception. L'Eternite.*

Last night the *bicyclettes* racing around and around the square in the heat. Colors. Names: Chambord, Bilot et Fils. Flags. The *bicyclettes* whirling. A microphone, trophies. Who can make sense of any of it? I miss her.

If I turn my head I can see the great vaulted entrance. Bright light pours in. Luminous vegetables and fruit. Let it be enough for now, I ask the Virgin.

Two children hold a white linen underneath the priest to catch fallen hosts.

"*Le Corps du Christ.*"

"Amen."

"*Le Corps du Christ.*"

"Amen."

Dimanche and the bells. I pass a striped cat pressed against a window screen. A red rose pulsing. In the market are *framboise* Vence, *anchois, artichaux violets.* I hold the large, globed artichoke, the glowing tomatoes. I go into the *patisserie* for brioche. People buy *gateaux.* They'll walk down the peaceful streets this afternoon. "*Bonne apres-midi, bonne promenade, bon appetit,*" they're all saying. Then suddenly all is quiet.

Dejeuner behind closed shutters. All the streets of France empty. The sound of silverware, low voices. The civility of midday. I'll never know what they say.

I wish I had someone to bring *gateau* to—or a tarte citron.

Dimanche—our day to talk on the phone. You are my dove, I will tell her. My *colombe d'or.* You are my *framboise* Vence. How the day revolves around the hour of the call. How the day dissolves in white wine and Cassis.

Three o'clock. It is three in the afternoon here, but it is only nine in the morning there and she's probably just waking up. She's probably just stepped from her bath. She's wearing my white bathrobe. She's opening the Sunday paper. She's petting our cat. She's drinking too much coffee.

I love her.

When I dial the number I am already drunk. A thousand centimes, those beautiful coins I still haven't learned to spend, fall from my pockets. They shine like gold.

The miracle of her voice inside this glass booth. It's a shock every time. The miracle of her voice as I look out at the olive trees, fig trees. The figs just beginning. I tell her all about my week. I can't stop talking. English! I tell her about the Arab music that sometimes snakes around the corner of the old town.

I tell her about French pizza, about the *bicyclettes*. She is silent. Talk to me, I say. She can't. *"Qu'est-ce que c'est?"* I ask. "What is it?"

"I'm seeing someone else."

"No."

"I met her at a party."

"I don't believe you."

"It's true.

And then she begins. She says she can't stand the separations anymore. She says she can't believe she put up with so much. She says something about all my affairs. Something about double standards. She can't go on. She says she will always love me but she can no longer be a slave to my genius.

"My *genius*. What genius?"

"I can't live with your genius," she says again.

I can't match this voice with anyone. I can't reconcile the thing she is saying with the brilliant day. Through the glass I watch women with *gateaux*. Children. Flowers. The figs just beginning. All I can say is I don't believe it. "I don't believe you. *Je ne le crois pas.*"

She says I never loved her enough. She says I always put my work first. She says I've been very cruel. She begins to list my crimes. But I scarcely remember being that woman.

And then she is gone. Somewhere far off there are more bells. Centimes fly around my head like some incomprehensible future. I close my eyes and see colors. Last night the *bicyclettes*.

There's very little to say about the days that immediately follow. They are filled with what one might expect—the usual anger, sadness, paralysis.

Melancholy music on the French radio. Stupid songs that are capable of making me cry. Every song seems to be for me, even the ones that I can't translate. I understand minor chords, they are the same in every language, the longing voice, the voice lingering on the single half-note. Even the most sentimental, the most terrible songs move me to tears. I cry all the time. I keep the shutters closed.

Is that rain? No, it is the water boiling.

Is that the magpie? No, my God, that is me.

I am here without rain or birds or light. I am here alone with my list of considerable crimes. I left often, sometimes for months, to write. I seduced her brother. I slept with the next-door neighbor. I slept with everyone. Once I even fell in love. It is true that often I was cruel. She said I was selfish, that I never thought of anything but writing. I was too moody. Too sad. I wasn't happy enough about my achievements. I was never satisfied. I never took good enough care of her.

I am so weary of my life. I will live to be old I think. I will live to pay for every crime. Even the minor ones. Among the minor ones: I never learned to drive. I always messed up my bankbook. I wouldn't talk about the movies after the light came up again. I couldn't talk about them, I don't know why.

I have given my whole life over to the creation of beauty. That it should come to this, I think. A woman in a white bed crying and listening to the songs from America with their awful lyrics, their few ugly notes.

In my notebook I write: "She was afraid of the woman and her many moods. Her unpredictability. Her often volatile and violent nature. All her silences and retreats. The first woman mistook this quality in the second woman for genius."

A long history of manic depression.

I am all alone in my big bed. I eat a bit from my consoling loaf of brioche each day. The answer to the question all the men ask me is *oui. Je suis toute seule.*

You bruise easily, I think. You go under.

That the pursuit of beauty should sometimes have to look like this: a woman, a bed, a half-eaten loaf of brioche, many empty wine bottles, a swirl of vomit, the radio playing its handful of sad songs.

She sleeps badly when she sleeps at all, wakes herself from

every dream, refuses to dream anymore, and is always up to hear the magpies tearing apart the dawn.

After many days, she doesn't know how many, she decides to get on a bus and go somewhere. Get up now she thinks to herself or not at all. One wants to be in love through this—with anything, and she chooses Nice, or it chooses her, that deliriously beautiful city by the sea. If anything is certain it is this, every time Nice will take her breath away. She stares out at the incredible color of the *Mediteraneé.* She hears the sound of water over stones. She sits there hour after hour. She counts the palms on the magnificent promenade. She counts all the blue chairs.

From the guidebook she reads Nice industries are olive oil and flowers, perfume, crystallized fruit and macaroni and she thinks what could be better than this?

Italians pass. They say *"Nizza,"* as if in a dream.

She walks into the old city. She walks into the countless churches. She writes: "I step from light to darkness to light. All the angels watch me. All the angels of Europe, tell me, yield some clue as to why this cannot be—this loving one person hard in one place. Angels of France, comfort me."

She cries easily.

She follows a young woman into the new city. Into American Express. She overhears her changing money, picking up a ticket. An American. She follows her into an English-language bookstore. Watches her pick up Walt Whitman, William Carlos Williams, Wallace Stevens. She is in love with all the right people. She follows her into the Prisunic. Watches her buy plastic dolphin combs for her hair. Next she goes into the market, asks for avocados. She explains she is from *Californie* and she is *un petit peu* homesick.

I walk up to her. I tell her I am an American. She's pleased. She has come from Cologne where she still has some family. She is just passing through. She tells me she is a writer. She writes poetry. I think her hair is the kind of blond that shines in your hands.

I tell her I too am a writer. I tell her about my book, the first one. She says that sounds just like a book she knows and she says the name. It is the same book I tell her. She can't believe it. Because we are in Nice, we have a Salade Nicoise together. We drink a bottle of wine. She is a little in love with the idea of me. She loves the intrigue. She talks about Nice. How it seems arranged around desire. That mild and beautiful city.

I ask her where she is staying.

"The Hotel Rivoli," she says. "You would like it there." Because she knows my book, she thinks she knows me. And she is partially right.

"Let's see if you are right about the Hotel Rivoli."

She laughs wildly. Suddenly she feels like she is in over her head. Her courage disappears. "Or maybe we should have another drink in the old city."

"No."

"OK."

We enter the Hotel Rivoli, only a few streets away.

She quotes poetry for me. "Although I do not hope to turn again./ Although I do not hope./ Although I do not hope to turn."

"T. S. Eliot," I say. I love my language. I feel home in my throat.

She says next:

> *Sun, sunflower,*
> *coltsfoot on the roadside,*
> *a goldfinch, the sign*
> *that says Yield, her hair*
> *cat's eyes, his hunger*
> *and a yellow bicycle.*

"That's Robert Hass," she tells me.

We order champagne.

Is it the sea you hear in me,
Its dissatisfactions?
Or the voice of nothing,
  that was your madness

Love is a shadow.
How you lie and cry after it
Listen: these are its hooves;
  it has gone off like a horse.

"Sylvia Plath."

I cry. We drink.

"I thought you would be the type to cry. Your first book was so sad."

"The second too," I say. "It will be out soon." I spent three years writing that book, I think, preparing myself for every kind of betrayal, every sort of defection, and still I was unprepared.

I take the dolphins from her hair. For a moment this young Californian feels she is in the first book. The one I love would have called this one of my many abuses of power.

I miss her.

"I've never been with a woman before," she says.

"I know," I say. "I've been watching you all day. But I think you'd like to be . . ."

"Yes, I guess."

"With me." "Yes."

"My God," she says. "My God," she says later that night. "No wonder men are crazy for women." She is the type that talks. "Women are sexy, and soft and warm and wet and incredible!" She is used to describing everything. And I am on my knees this time, and she is already screaming.

In the morning an old woman brings *deux café cremes, deux croissants.*

She comes in quickly, slows up, and smiles. She has seen

stranger things than two naked women in *un petit lit* together. The room smells familiar to me. There's a warm breeze.

We walk into beautiful Nice. The city opens like she did. "Nice is golden. Nice is pale green and pink. Nice is the most incredible sea blue." I am delighted to be speaking my language. "It is the person you love. It is the day off. It is macaroni. It is *socca*. Nice is pressed glass and polka dots. The fins of fish. The Galeries Lafayette."

Nice is golden. She is golden.

"It is sex with women," she says. It is *vin rose*. And champagne. City of splendor. City of gold.

We go to the beach. The French boys on the promenade wear T-shirts that say "surf, surf," and "rowing team," and "no problem." We laugh. She quotes Rimbaud for me. She tells me the French she knows. She tells me that fruits and flowers are feminine.

We do her last-minute shopping in the Galeries Lafayette. We buy lipsticks and lingerie. She's leaving this evening.

On the beach she quotes me one more thing.

> *The palm at the end of the mind,*
> *Beyond the last thought, rises*
> *In the bronze decor,*
>
> *A gold-feathered bird*
> *Sings in the palm, without*
>   *human meaning,*
> *Without human feeling, a foreign song.*

She kisses away my tears, salty as the sea. "Good-bye young poet," I say as she gets onto the plane.

Across the blue envelope of sky I write, "Be safe, small angel, take care, write well."

She's got dolphins in her hair.

Once she has lain next to water she is drawn back to it again and again. Any kind of water. The next day in Vence she goes to the municipal pool. *La piscine municipale.*

She watches the French swim. Notes their preference for the breaststroke. She watches a woman in a black bathing suit light a cigarette. She feels the pervasive and strange eroticism in these days. The slight breeze presses her toward men she doesn't know. Men whose language she can't speak.

She is wearing her Chinese hat. She is holding her open notebook. She had come to France to write about water, but since the phone call she works erratically, goes to the *piscine,* stares out at the chlorine rectangle bordered by cypress and willow and olives. She studies the perfect white tiles. She watches the relatively well-behaved French children do what they do.

"Regarde!" they shout. *"Regardez-moi!"*

"Nage avec les jambes!" a man calls out to his son.

She observes the particular habits of the French. The young at the poolside talking. She's beginning to recognize the specific beauty of these people.

She writes in her notebook, "Often she tried to quell sexual desire with a long swim in the pool. Often she tried to curb despair there." "You bruise easily," she writes, "you go under."

She writes in her notebook:

> *An arc of talent.*
> *An arc of sadness.*
> *A wave.*
> *A chlorine blue wave.*
> *A black bathing suit.*
> *Thunder.*
> *The perfect stroke of the swimmer.*
> *Desire.*
> *The threat of rain.*
> *Then rain.*

Desire perfects the perfect stroke
  of the swimmer.

She doesn't know what it means. She watches a man slowly lower himself into water. She is alone.

Often she tried to hold back despair, stave off depression, with another affair. Impossible to explain.

Her mind drifts. They did things together, she thinks. They had fun. They went to a goat farm. They had a Portuguese dinner. They saw something called "The Tale of Lear." They caught a fish. She doesn't know why she writes it all down. Soon they would have been together, here. They thought they might have a child. It's useless to think of.

She yearns for the kind of beauty that could break even the heart that is already broken. She looks for it everywhere—on paper, at the pool.

She lowers herself into water. She begins to swim. Desire perfects the perfect stroke of the swimmer. They went to a restaurant called Chez Jacqueline, once. They played the same record over and over. They watched their friend, in a white room, die. They went to see a beautiful black-and-white film. It was German. Bruno Ganz was an angel.

A child floats by. It's useless to think of.

My mother writes: "Dearest Catherine, the Fourth of July celebration is over. We had grilled, butterflied leg of lamb, parsleyed red potatoes, broccoli and for dessert a large flag made of cake and ice cream. Everyone seemed to enjoy it. You were the only one missing. Everyone left quite early on July fifth. It was nice to see them and they all seemed quite well.

"I've been spending a lot of time quietly watering the gardens. We haven't had rain in a month and the weather has been hot. Watering is verboten, but I can't bear to watch it all dry up. The lawn is brown, that's bad enough. There are hollyhocks, sentinels of white, red and pink in the garden. Everybody admires them. Also for the first time Jacob's Ladder has bloomed. It is a cluster of delicate purple flowers with yellow centers and the leaves are fernlike. The orange butterfly weed is in full bloom as are the Gliosa Daisies. They look like small sunflowers and make me think of you in the South of France. . . ."

I miss my mother. I wish she would come here.

I go to Arles by train. Van Gogh walked there one hundred years ago and that is good enough for me. On the train I write her letters I won't send. I sit in a cage with five German men who look out at the sea and then to me. I don't know what anything means. I never used to look for meaning, but now I feel that need. I realize I am already braced for the next disaster.

I have called in advance and reserved a room in a hotel on "La Place du Docteur Pomme." I suppose I have come to try to get well. No weeping women here, I think, putting away the letters I have begun to her.

I'm the last one off the train. A young woman looks at me and immediately begins to cry. "What is it?" I ask.

"You are the last person on the train," she says in French. "He is not coming."

"Perhaps he will be on the train tomorrow," I say.

"*Non.*" She cries and cries. "He has said that if he was not on this train it would mean he is not coming, never coming."

I think to myself this is such a sad life.

We decide to go to a café together. She orders a *l'eau minerale*. It turns out he is her first lover, a painter she had been modeling for. The man is *Anglais* and she has learned some English from him. She says that her heart is breaking.

I tell her the heart is more fragile than fruit. It can't be handled tenderly enough.

She smiles. "You are very kind," she says.

She was born in the Carmargue. She is seventeen. One could easily understand the desire to paint her—the thick dark hair, the full breasts and hips. She hopes one day to model in Paris. It is her dream. "I will show you the town," she decides.

Caesar made Arles a Roman colony, and the whole town seems like a vast museum. It is hers and she walks through it, majestic and damaged. A statue. We go to the Cloisters, the amphitheater, the Arenes. At the Arenes she says, "They have bullfights here. Spanish music plays. Sometimes I can smell blood." We walk along the Rhone.

At dinner we sit at the Forum, a huge open square bordered by plane trees. Small white lights are strung up everywhere. It's still hot. A French man with a guitar sings a Simon and Garfunkel song, "I swear I was so lonely that I took some comfort there." It's an odd thing to hear.

She talks more about the man. "He is a very great painter, I think," she says. But it makes her sad to say much more. "Tell me something else," I say. She tells me she rode wild horses as a girl. "The horses are born brown," she says, "and they turn white when they are grown. They are very beautiful. Sauvage. There are great pink and orange birds there," she says. "My father grows rice. You would like it. Maybe some day we could go."

Il fait chaud. She has already said she is most comfortable without clothes.

"I must go," I say, "to the Place du Docteur Pomme. But tomorrow."

For a long time the next morning I watch the concierge feeding birds. Her outstretched fingers scatter crumbs. Every gesture in this light feels enormous, archetypal. I walk to the woman's house. Her name is Dominique. *"Bon matin,* Catherine. We drink *café* on a terrace in bright light. *"Il fait trop chaud,"* she says.

She tells me last night she cried herself to sleep.

"How did it happen, with the man?"

"Un moment." She goes into the house for a minute. "I was wearing this." She shows me a bright blue silk robe. "He bought

it for me. All the way from China. He began to paint, but he did not like my pose. He said to try putting my hand here" and she put it between her breasts. "Move in here," he said, and she put her hand on her thigh. Then between her legs. "He asked me to make it look like I was touching myself there. He said if I wanted I could touch myself. He kissed me. I had never made love before. He knew this and kissed me just slightly. Barely, barely brushing my lips. *Comme ca.*" And she shows me. "It was like that that he kissed me at first. Later he would bruise my lips, the way he would kiss me.

"We went back to the pose. My hand here."

"Did you like that?"

"I liked it most when he was watching and I was thinking of that gentle kiss, *oui*. Later it was different. I longed for the time when there was only that smallest of kisses."

We go for a walk. I take her to my rented room on La Place du Docteur Pomme.

"Once he had me pose with another woman. She was fair like the English are. Like you. At first I was jealous of her. He was very wise. He saw this. He told me to touch her neck gently like the kiss had been. He said it must seem relaxed, natural. We became friends, the fair woman and me. I grew to like her very much. She was twenty-eight, older. She said she had been modeling for eight years. In Paris. That often afterwards she made love with them. But I never felt as happy as when I was touching her neck, gazing into her face in our pose."

"Where is she now?"

"She was about to marry. She lived with a painter in Paris. One day I will go to Paris.

"Have you ever modeled?"

"No. *Je suis ecrivaine.*"

"*Vraiment?* What do you write?"

"Stories about love and then love taken away."

"They are sad, then?"

"Yes. They are sad stories."

"I love sad stories. Stories that make me cry. I don't know why." She thought of the painter. His name was Nigel. "You know then about sadness?"

"I am twenty-eight. I am the same age as the woman whose neck you touched. It is old enough to know a great deal about sadness."

"You are more beautiful than that woman. Don't be sad now."

My hair is pinned up. She dares to touch my neck. She brushes my lips with her mouth again. "I know nothing," she whispers, "except that Nigel had me touch her neck, touch myself and then put my finger to her lips. That is all."

"Like this?"

"*Oui*. I did it for the painting. It was my work. But I could never forget after that. Even though I felt *honte*."

"What is that?"

"*Ce n'est pas bon*. It's hard to explain." She puts her dark finger to my lips. We hold the pose a long time.

I take each finger gently, gently into my mouth and she lets out a small sigh.

"*Un petit gout*," I say. She nods. She is sweet like the ripe melons of Cavillon. "*Tiens.*"

"*Un petit gout, s'il te plait.*" Her robe falls open. Her dark body gives off an extraordinary light. She seems to glisten.

She touches my neck again. She applies just the slightest pressure. Her touch tells me she wants more. She wants my mouth on her breasts. I touch her round belly. She nods. She wants my mouth to descend to that triangle, it's luxurious, dark. And she too needs a small taste. She grows. She grows wild. She turns from a brown horse into a white one. I pull her magnificent mane, press her between her thighs. Ride into light.

"Dominique."

Every tree bears fruit here. All afternoon we eat plums, figs. "It's my birthday," she says.

I sing her the birthday song, off-key. She laughs. "You are so lovely," I say. She is eighteen.

I run my wrists under cool water in the terrible heat of the room.

In the night she says, "Perhaps you will write a story about me. It will be a little sad this story—but mostly no."

Something opens that cannot be closed. Heat opens us further. Bees. There's an incredible lushness. "You are so delicious," I say.

"*Et toi!*" I can scarcely believe what ripens in me.

Overnight the Sirocco had come driving the Sahara into France, into our throats and onto the hoods of the cars of Vence. I write her name—Elena—in the sand. The umbrellas at La Regence fly off their axis. I am happy to be back in this town I have begun to memorize. Because to know the pattern in the door or the design of stones in the street or the gratings and railings in every kind of light helps, a little.

She says there is someone else, and suddenly everything is sand.

I step into the garden of the Hotel de Provence and order a Pernod. I can still smell the woman from Arles in my hair, on my skin. I'm alone here; no one else in the garden and I like that.

"It's my birthday," she whispers in my ear. "Do this for me. Don't move much or someone will see. Shh—pretend you are modeling. Now move your hand to your breast. Now move your hand again. I'll be watching you," she says. "I'll be touching your neck." I open my legs, moving only slightly. The tip of my finger on the tip of my clitoris.

I wonder if someone upstairs parting the curtain watches this trembling woman as she touches herself in the *jardin* of the Hotel de Provence. I have fantasized too precisely. A man appears out of nowhere. He walks through arbors, under trellises.

"*Excuse-moi,*" he says, "but I have to know, what is that scent? It is so familiar to me."

"*Je ne comprend pas,*" I say.

The wind picks up suddenly. The wind stirs up everything. There's sand in my eyes. I hear the voice of an old woman in the next villa shouting in English, "We'll all be blown to bits."

"*Ton parfum,*" he says. "*Qu'est-ce que c'est?*" He asks to sit. I nod.

"I ask because I am in the business of perfume. And it is making me crazy—the name for that scent."

"*La Jeune Arlesienne,*" I say.

Inseminating the Cows

Diane Frank

With a wild and tender look in his eye
he told me that he is the one
who inseminates the cows.
At the only dairy in Iowa
where the cows have names like
Starfire Sari,
Utopia,
Aranyani,
and Eternal St. Faye,
they use semen from a bull with
87 daughters,
all good milk producers, he said.
You have to do it at the precise moment
when they are ready,
about 12 hours after they go into heat.
How do you know, I asked him.
He smiled. He said,
most of them go into heat together.
They play in rings.
and even mount each other.
Utopia usually gets them started.
He said their personality totally changes.
Sita, for example,
normally a shy girl,
got so excited when she was in heat last year,
that she repeatedly mounted the bull.
He winked at me. He said,
I loved to watch them playing
but never saw them complete.

The bull had several children,
but they must have mated in the evening
or in a secret place.
Maybe he was a woman, I said,
in a previous life, and still shy.
But they sold the bull last autumn,
and now, he proudly told me,
they use semen from the best prize bull
in the country.
Ten dollars a straw.
Frozen to 323 degrees below zero
in liquid nitrogen
and ready to go.
After the cows go into heat,
you check the mucus.
When they're ready, it's long and stringy
and falls completely down to the ground.
First you put a glove on
all the way up to the shoulder,
and put your hand up her anus
to feel the uterus.
It feels a certain way when they're ready,
firm and toned,
and you know.
Then you take a straw in your other hand,
and gently put it up her vagina.
You have to find the cervix.
It's wet, hard, and cartilaginous
like a woman's. A human cervix
feels something like the bottom of your nose.
Well, a cow's is something like that, he said.
You have to find the opening.
which is very small
and sometimes difficult.
Then you insert the straw

in exactly the right place,
deposit the semen,
and you massage her uterus
for a while with your other hand
so it will take.
Then you know the act is complete
and you leave the cows dreaming
of strong bulls and loving afterplay.
As he tells me, his farmer's hands
are around me
and he massages my left foot
in slow circles
as we lie on my Japanese bed.
I wonder how many men
could describe a human woman's body
with such tenderness and accuracy.
I wonder if he would make
as good a father for human babies.
And he is wondering
about the shapes of everything
inside my white Victoria's Secret nightgown.

Waking Up
Twice

James Clark
Anderson

Blue-black of a winter morning.
Six o'clock. Between ghosts of houses
the lighter horizontal of the street.
We make an attempt at waking, open
our eyes, our covers, our untried hopes,
taking a first breath of the great air
around the bed. I look at you, you look
through the softly glowing rectangle of light
we remember will lead us to the living room.
Get up. No one has to say it. We move
from darkness into an orange-yellow glow,
toward a copper lamp hanging from the ceiling.
If ever we move from here, this room,
this light, this time of waking up with you,
not conscious or intelligible, is what
I want to bring with us to the next world.
Walking behind I feel the swish of your nightgown
between us, it moves with your rhythm, and so what
if I have a place to go in less than an hour.
We have two cups of tea, a bedside stand
for them to sit on while we undress again.
Undressing again, I stare at your breasts
against the flat, gray-blue of sky
there in the window now. Your shapes, my own,
we lie down, closing our eyes into the shapeless
ocean of movement under the sheet, not sleep,

not rest or conversation, only the wash
and wish of arms lightly over shoulders, hands
following a smoothness down, the belly, thighs
tightening, opening, tightening, opening.

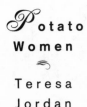

Potato Women

Teresa Jordan

To the sad lowing of cows at evensong, the women pick up a few last potatoes and stash them in burlap bags. They push back their head scarves and rub the sweat off their brows. One brings her hand to her mouth and sucks on the fleshy part of her thumb. It tastes of earth and roots; it tastes of her own salt. She casts her shovel in the earth and it stands upright as a suitor. It will wait like that until morning when she will come back for it. The thought of it, standing alone as if waiting for some sort of encouragement, makes her feel powerful. She laughs and taps it before she turns for home. She has children in the town, staying with their grandmother, her mother, a very old woman who sits by the fire all day and dreams through her tired blue eyes of digging potatoes. The children are good around Grandmama because she is gentle, and they don't take advantage of her blindness. They play quietly outside and one comes in from time to time to touch her on the hand and say "It is me, Grandmama, it is Pepe," or, "It is Nina." "We have been picking tulips." "We have been throwing the stick to the dog." "We have been eating custard at Carlotta's house, and her mother said there was plenty."

The old grandmama likes the sound of the children's voices, and she likes the way they keep coming back to her and letting her know where they are, what they have been doing. Her own daughter had been angry and wild: Who would have thought such sweetness could come out of her womb.

The old woman had never wondered why her daughter chose Ivan. She would have, even as old as she was, if she could have kept his eye. He was a black-haired man, dark and strong, broad-chinned, fire-eyed. He was a soldier and he always carried his rifle in a scabbard slung across his back. It was as much a part of him as a baby in a sling is to its mother during the first year of its life. He seemed as gentle as a mother, and as fierce. The old woman remembered wondering if he took off the rifle when he touched her daughter, and when she saw her daughter's belly swell long before they talked of marriage, and she saw the fire in her daughter's eyes calm into a more steady sort of light she thought: My daughter has chosen well. He will keep her strong.

This was a small village. No one judged the daughter for the size of her belly at the wedding feast, and everyone brought gifts when the baby boy was born. Ivan was away at some war or another, but when he got word he headed home. He arrived in the middle of the night with a sweet potato. He cooked it himself in a pot on the stove and fed his wife little bites of it, dripping with butter, from a spoon. He held his son and then he undressed and held the child against his nakedness. He touched his own rough skin and he touched the tender white skin of his son and he touched the stronger skin of his son's mother and they all lay together naked and the baby started to cry. The mother put him to her breast and then she pulled Ivan to the other one and Ivan laid his rifle aside and that night he fathered another son.

Ivan was one of those men everyone knew would leave a widow early on, but the grandmama's daughter never quit thinking of him after the news arrived that he had killed three men before he was shot from behind. She thought of him in the fields while she dug potatoes, and she thought of him as she walked weary back to town. She thought of her seven children, of the three boys who came first and the four girls who came after. She had given the oldest daughter her father's gun because she knew the girl would understand it best. There is a wisdom in the oldest daughter; not greater than the wisdom in the oldest son but different, and the daughters always need their fathers' weapons more than the sons do.

The grandmama is dozing again and wakes to her daughter's step, to the smell of fresh dug potatoes and clean dirt. She hears her daughter splashing water in the basin and rubbing the calluses on her hands. She listens as little particles of dirt loosen from the skin. The old woman's hearing had grown more acute as she lost her sight, and she can hear tiny particles float through the soapy water and land softly on the bottom of the basin. She can distinguish the sounds made by different textures of skin. Sometimes the sounds are so loud and so varied she wants to cry out: Stop touching! But there are so few pleasures in the world, she holds her tongue.

She listens as her daughter stands at the window and dries her hands on the dish towel. "Mother," the daughter says, "are you hungry?"

"Not so much," the mother says.

"We will have potatoes," the daughter says.

"I know," her mother answers. "The children ate egg custard earlier. Are you very tired?"

The mother knows that her daughter is always tired now, and that she goes to bed each night and dreams of Ivan. "You should marry," she says, but her daughter doesn't answer. "I have heard so many men ask you to marry, to let them feed your children." But still the daughter is silent.

The old woman knows that her daughter lies with other men; she knows each time it happens, even if they lie together in another village, because the song of their skin is so loud. But she knows, too, that her daughter keeps some tiny dark part of herself sealed off. Seed never enters her daughter's womb: the old woman would hear the shattering of glass and sorrow.

The daughter puts potatoes on the stove and leaves the cottage. The grandmama knows she will go to the baths and soak. The grandmama used to do the same when she was younger, and sometimes now her daughter takes her along and leads her down the mossy steps.

The old woman listens, in her dozing, for the sound of her daughter's apron falling, her skirt folding heavily across the back of a chair, her toes touching the water, and the water sliding along her salt-caked calves and up her thighs. She hears her daughter settle on the old green stone in the corner, she hears her close her eyes. The old woman knows that in the dreaming her daughter settles into, Ivan returns. The grandmama listens to nipples stiffen in the water, she hears the moaning hum. It's good the children have eaten custard, she thinks as she settles into her own widow's dreams. She is hardly hungry anyway.

First Desire/
First Time

Rachel Guido
deVries

again. The Hudson begins its watery curve.
Lay low. I tremble with longing. Maple and aspen
along the shoreline tremble too, leaves all silvery
at seven. I fill up with juice for the life of it.
The green of me stretches, lithe, a sapling. I
long for you. Though I've not yet touched you
taste bone sweet, your scent is in my sleep. I wake
wet and hungry, my mouth a dream between your thighs.
The river runs fierce just here. In its reflection
trees rustle and lean, ablaze.

Little Fires

Rachel Guido
deVries

Come on. I want to climb your body like a tree,
rest beneath your big breasts, slide my mouth
slow like a fish floating in a lake. I can
dart my tongue like a silver minnow all shiny
with stars inside you. Along the last curve,
where the hottest darkness is, I'll leave
a single star for later. Hours after I
re-enter the sky, you'll know its silvery
feel. Watch for the moon to rise,
for its companions to fill the night. I want
to fill you up like that, hot stars dancing
on my tongue like little fires I burn inside you.

Late May at Little Rapids

D. Nurkse

We love each other
once with closed eyes
once with open eyes
then we lie and let the wind
touch us and at dawn
the great silence falls
and we're lost in it
though we still hear our voices
explaining how we'll live together.

Evergreen
in Summer

D. Nurkse

She was naked
except for a line of dirt
under her little fingernail.
The pool she'd swum in
still trembled slightly.
An owl called
in daylight, then another.
We were in the spruce forest.
Looking up from under her
I saw a white cloud
between her neck and shoulder.
I closed my eyes.
When I looked again
the sky was empty.
Brown needles clung
to the lines of my palm.

Spirits

Peter and the Wolf

_~_

Angela
Carter

At length the grandeur of the mountains becomes monotonous; with familiarity, the landscape ceases to provoke awe and wonder and the traveler sees the alps with the indifferent eye of those who always live there. Above a certain line, no trees grow. Shadows of clouds move across the bare alps as freely as the clouds themselves move across the sky.

A girl from a village on the lower slopes left her widowed mother to marry a man who lived up in the empty places. Soon she was pregnant. In October, there was a severe storm. The old woman knew her daughter was near her time and waited for a message but none arrived. After the storm passed, the old woman went up to see for herself, taking her grown son with her because she was afraid.

From a long way off, they saw no smoke rising from the chimney. Solitude yawned round them. The open door banged backwards and forwards on its hinges. Solitude engulfed them. There were traces of wolf-dung on the floor so they knew wolves had been in the house but left the corpse of the young mother alone although of her baby nothing was left except some mess that showed it had been born. Nor was there a trace of the son-in-law but a gnawed foot in a boot.

They wrapped the dead in a quilt and took it home with them. Now it was late. The howling of the wolves mutilated the approaching silence of the night.

Winter came with icy blasts, when everyone stays indoors and stokes the fire. The old woman's son married the black-smith's daughter and she moved in with them. The snow melted and it was spring. By the next Christmas, there was a bouncing grandson. Time passed. More children came.

When the eldest grandson, Peter, reached his seventh summer, he was old enough to go up the mountain with his father, as the men did every year, to let the goats feed on the young grass. There Peter sat in the new sunlight, plaiting the straw for baskets, until he saw the thing he had been taught most to fear advancing silently along the lea of an outcrop of rock. Then another wolf, following the first one.

If they had not been the first wolves he had ever seen, the boy would not have inspected them so closely, their plush, gray pelts, of which the hairs are tipped with white, giving them a ghostly look, as if they were on the point of dissolving at the edges; their sprightly, plumey tails; their acute, inquisitive masks.

Then Peter saw that the third wolf was a prodigy, a marvel, a naked one, going on all fours, as they did, but hairless as regards the body although hair grew around its head.

The sight of this bald wolf so fascinated him that he would have lost his flock, perhaps himself been eaten and certainly been beaten to the bone for negligence had not the goats themselves raised their heads, snuffed danger, and run off, bleating and whinnying, so that the men came firing guns, making hullabaloo, scaring the wolves away.

His father was too angry to listen to what Peter said. He cuffed Peter around the head and sent him home. His mother was feeding this year's baby. His grandmother sat at the table, shelling peas into a pot.

"There was a little girl with the wolves, Granny," said Peter. Why was he so sure it had been a little girl? Perhaps because her hair was so long, so long and lively. "A little girl about my age, from her size," he said.

His grandmother threw a flat pod out of the door so the chickens could peck it up.

"I saw a little girl with the wolves," he said.

His grandmother tipped water into the pot, got up from the table, and hung the pot of peas on the hook over the fire. There wasn't time, that night, but, next morning, very early, she herself took the boy back up the mountain.

"Tell your father what you told me."

They went to look at the wolves' tracks. On a bit of dampish ground they found a print, not like that of a dog's pad, much less like that of a child's footprint, yet Peter worried and puzzled over it until he made sense of it.

"She was running on all fours with her arse stuck up in the air . . . therefore . . . she'd put all her weight on the ball of her foot, wouldn't she? And splay out her toes, see . . . like that."

He went barefoot in summer, like all the village children; he inserted the ball of his own foot in the print, to show his father what kind of mark he would have made if he, too, always ran on all fours.

"No use for a heel, if you run that way. So she doesn't have a heel-print. Stands to reason."

At last his father made a slow acknowledgment of Peter's powers of deduction, giving the child a veiled glance of disquiet. It was a clever child.

They soon found her. She was asleep. Her spine had grown so supple she could curl into a perfect C. She woke up when she heard them and ran, but somebody caught her with a sliding noose at the end of a rope; the noose over her head jerked tight and she fell to the ground with her eyes popping and rolling. A big, gray, angry bitch appeared out of nowhere but Peter's father blasted it to bits with his shotgun. The girl would have choked if the old woman hadn't taken her head on her lap and pulled the knot loose. The girl bit the grandmother's hand.

The girl scratched and fought until the men tied her wrists and ankles together with twine and slung her from a pole to carry her back to the village. Then she went limp. She didn't scream or shout, she didn't seem to be able to, she made only a few dull, guttural sounds in the back of her throat, and, though she did not seem to know how to cry, water trickled out of the corners of her eyes.

How burned she was by the weather! Bright brown all over; and how filthy she was! Caked with mud and dirt. And every inch of her chestnut hide was scored and scabbed with dozens of scars of sharp abrasions of rock and thorn. Her hair dragged on the ground as they carried her along; it was stuck with burrs and it was so dirty you could not see what color it might be. She was dreadfully verminous. She stank. She was so thin that all her ribs stuck out. The fine, plump, potato-fed boy was far bigger than she, although she was a year or so older.

Solemn with curiosity, he trotted behind her. Granny stumped alongside with her bitten hand wrapped up in her apron. Once the girl was dumped on the earth floor of her grandmother's house, the boy secretly poked at her left buttock with his forefinger, out of curiosity, to see what she felt like. She felt warm but hard. She did not so much as twitch when he touched her. She had given up the struggle; she lay trussed on the floor and pretended to be dead.

Granny's house had the one large room which, in winter, they shared with the goats. As soon as it caught a whiff of her, the big tabby mouser hissed like a pricked balloon and bounded up the ladder that went to the hayloft above. Soup smoked on the fire and the table was laid. It was now about suppertime but still quite light; night comes late on the summer mountain.

"Untie her," said the grandmother.

Her son wasn't willing at first but the old woman would not be denied, so he got the breadknife and cut the rope round the girl's ankles. All she did was kick, but when he cut the rope round her wrists, it was as if he had let a fiend loose. The on-lookers ran out of the door, the rest of the family ran for the ladder to the hayloft but Granny and Peter both ran to the door, to shoot the bolt, so she could not get out.

The trapped one knocked round the room. Bang—over went the table. Crash, tinkle—the supper dishes smashed. Bang, crash, tinkle the dresser fell forward upon the hard white shale of crockery it shed in falling. Over went the meal barrel and she coughed, she sneezed like a child sneezes, no different, and then she bounced around on fear-stiffened legs in a white cloud until the flour settled on everything like a magic powder that made everything strange. Her first frenzy over, she squatted a moment, questing with her long nose and then began to make little rushing sorties, now here, now there, snapping and yelping and tossing her bewildered head.

She never rose up on two legs; she crouched, all the time, on her hands and tiptoes, yet it was not quite like crouching, for you could see how all fours came naturally to her as though she had made a different pact with gravity than we have, and you could see, too, how strong the muscles in her thighs had grown on the mountain, how taut the twanging arches of her feet, and that indeed, she only used her heels when she sat back on her haunches. She growled; now and then she coughed out those intolerable, thick grunts of distress. All you could see of her rolling eyes were the whites, which were the bluish, glaring white of snow.

Several times, her bowels opened, apparently involuntarily. The kitchen smelled like a privy yet even her excrement was different to ours, the refuse of raw, strange, unguessable, wicked feeding, shit of a wolf.

Oh, horror!

She bumped into the hearth, knocked over the pan hanging from the hook and the spilled contents put out the fire. Hot soup scalded her forelegs. Shock of pain. Squatting on her hindquarters, holding the hurt paw dangling piteously from its wrist before her, she howled, in high, sobbing arcs.

Even the old woman, who had contracted with herself to love the child of her dead daughter, was frightened when she heard the girl howl.

Peter's heart gave a hop, a skip, so that he had a sensation of falling; he was not conscious of his own fear because he could not take his eyes off the sight of the crevice of her girl-child's sex, that was perfectly visible to him as she sat there square on the base of her spine. The night was now as dark as, at this season, it would go—which is to say, not very dark; a white thread of moon hung in the blond sky at the top of the chimney so that it was neither dark nor light indoors yet the boy could see her intimacy clearly, as if by its own phosphorescence. It exercised an absolute fascination upon him.

Her lips opened up as she howled so that she offered him, without her own intention or volition, a view of a set of Chinese boxes of whorled flesh that seemed to open one upon another into herself, drawing him into an inner, secret place in which destination perpetually receded before him, his first, devastating, vertiginous intimation of infinity.

She howled.

And went on howling until, from the mountain, first singly, then in a complex polyphony, answered at last voices in the same language.

She continued to howl, though now with a less tragic resonance.

Soon it was impossible for the occupants of the house to deny to themselves that the wolves were descending on the village in a pack.

Then she was consoled, sank down, laid her head on her forepaws so that her hair trailed in the cooling soup and so closed up her forbidden book without the least notion she had ever opened it or that it was banned. Her heavy eyelids closed on her brown, bloodshot eyes. The household gun hung on a nail over the fireplace where Peter's father had put it when he came in but when the man set his foot on the top rung of the ladder in order to come down for his weapon, the girl jumped up, snarling and showing her long yellow canines.

The howling outside was now mixed with the agitated dismay of the domestic beasts. All the other villagers were well locked up at home.

The wolves were at the door.

The boy took hold of his grandmother's uninjured hand. First the old woman would not budge but he gave her a good tug and she came to herself. The girl raised her head suspiciously but let them by. The boy pushed his grandmother up the ladder in front of him and drew it up behind them. He was full of nervous dread. He would have given anything to turn time back, so that he might have run, shouting a warning, when he first caught sight of the wolves, and never seen her.

The door shook as the wolves outside jumped up at it and the screws that held the socket of the bolt to the frame cracked, squeaked, and started to give. The girl jumped up, at that, and began to make excited little sallies back and forth in front of the door. The screws tore out of the frame quite soon. The pack tumbled over one another to get inside.

Dissonance. Terror. The clamor within the house was that of all the winds of winter trapped in a box. That which they feared most, outside, was now indoors with them. The baby in the hayloft whimpered and its mother crushed it to her breast as if the wolves might snatch this one away, too; but the rescue party had arrived only in order to collect their fosterling.

They left behind a riotous stench in the house, and white tracks of flour everywhere. The broken door creaked backwards and forwards on its hinges. Black sticks of dead wood from the extinguished fire were scattered on the floor.

Peter thought the old woman would cry, now, but she seemed unmoved. When all was safe, they came down the ladder one by one and, as if released from a spell of silence, burst into excited speech except for the mute old woman and the distraught boy. Although it was well past midnight, the daughter-in-law went to the well for water to scrub the wild smell out of the house. The broken things were cleared up and thrown away. Peter's father nailed the table and the dresser back together. The neighbors came out of their houses, full of amazement, the wolves had not taken so much as a chicken from the hen-coops, not snatched even a single egg.

People brought beer into the starlight, and schnapps made from potatoes, and snacks, because the excitement had made them hungry. That terrible night ended up in one big party but the grandmother would eat or drink nothing and went to bed as soon as her house was clean.

Next day, she went to the graveyard and sat for a while beside her daughter's grave but she did not pray. Then she came home and started chopping cabbage for the evening meal but had to leave off because her bitten hand was festering.

That winter, during the leisure imposed by the snow, after his grandmother's death, Peter asked the village priest to teach him to read the Bible. The priest gladly complied; Peter was the first of his flock who had ever expressed any interest in learning to read.

The boy became very pious, so much so that his family were startled and impressed. The younger children teased him and called him "Saint Peter" but that did not stop him sneaking off to church to pray whenever he had a spare moment. In Lent, he fasted to the bone. On Good Friday, he lashed himself. It was as if he blamed himself for the death of the old lady, as if he believed he had brought into the house the fatal infection that had taken her out of it. He was consumed by an imperious passion for atonement. Each night, he pored over his book by the flimsy candlelight, looking for a clue to grace, until his mother shooed him off to sleep.

But, as if to spite the four evangelists he nightly invoked to protect his bed, the nightmare regularly disordered his sleeps. He tossed and turned on the rustling straw pallet he shared with two little ones.

Delighted with Peter's precocious intelligence, the priest started to teach him Latin. Peter visited the priest as his duties with the herd permitted. When he was fourteen, the priest told his parents that Peter should now go to the seminary in the town in the valley where the boy would learn to become a priest himself. Rich in sons, they spared one to God, since his books and his praying made him a stranger to them. After the goats came down from the high pasture for the winter, Peter set off. It was October.

At the end of his first day's travel, he reached a river that ran from the mountain into the valley. The nights were already chilly; he lit himself a fire, prayed, ate bread and cheese his mother had packed for him and slept as well as he could. In spite of his eagerness to plunge into the white world of penance and devotion that awaited him, he was anxious and troubled for reasons he could not explain to himself.

In the first light, the light that no more than clarifies darkness like eggshells dropped in cloudy liquid, he went down to the river to drink and to wash his face. It was so still he could have been the one thing living.

Her forearms, her loins, and her legs were thick with hair and the hair on her head hung round her face in such a way that you could hardly make out her features. She crouched on the other side of the river. She was lapping up water so full of mauve light that it looked as if she were drinking up the dawn as fast as it appeared yet all the same the air grew pale while he was looking at her.

Solitude and silence; all still.

She could never have acknowledged that the reflection beneath her in the river was that of herself. She did not know she had a face; she had never known she had a face and so her face itself was the mirror of a different kind of consciousness than ours is, just as her nakedness, without innocence or display, was that of our first parents, before the Fall. She was hairy as Magdalen in the wilderness and yet repentance was not within her comprehension.

Language crumbled into dust under the weight of her speechlessness.

A pair of cubs rolled out of the bushes, cuffing one another. She did not pay them any heed.

The boy began to tremble and shake. His skin prickled. He

felt he had been made of snow and now might melt. He mumbled something, or sobbed.

She cocked her head at the vague, river-washed sound and the cubs heard it, too, left off tumbling and ran to burrow their scared heads in her side. But she decided, after a moment, there was no danger and lowered her muzzle, again, to the surface of the water that took hold of her hair and spread it out around her head.

When she finished her drink, she backed a few paces, shaking her wet pelt. The little cubs fastened their mouths on her dangling breasts.

Peter could not help it, he burst out crying. He had not cried since his grandmother's funeral. Tears rolled down his face and splashed on the grass. He blundered forward a few steps into the river with his arms held open, intending to cross over to the other side to join her in her marvelous and private grace, impelled by the access of an almost visionary ecstasy. But his cousin took fright at the sudden movement, wrenched her teats away from the cubs, and ran off. The squeaking cubs scampered behind. She ran on hands and feet as if that were the only way to run towards the high ground, into the bright maze of the uncompleted dawn.

When the boy recovered himself, he dried his tears on his sleeve, took off his soaked boots, and dried his feet and legs on the tail off his shirt. Then he ate something from his pack, he scarcely knew what, and continued on the way to the town; but what would he do at the seminary, now? For now he knew there was nothing to be afraid of.

He experienced the vertigo of freedom.

He carried his boots slung over his shoulder by the laces. They were a great burden. He debated with himself whether or not to throw them away but, when he came to a paved road, he had to put them on, although they were still damp.

The birds woke up and sang. The cool, rational sun surprised him; morning had broken on his exhilaration and the mountain now lay behind him. He looked over his shoulder and saw how, with distance, the mountain began to acquire a flat, two-dimensional look. It was already turning into a picture of itself, into the postcard hastily bought as a souvenir of childhood at a railway station or a border post, the newspaper cutting, the snapshot he would show in strange towns, strange cities, other countries he could not, at this moment, imagine, whose names he did not yet know, places where he would say, in strange languages, "That was where I spent my childhood. Imagine!"

He turned and stared at the mountain for a long time. He had lived in it for fourteen years but he had never seen it before as it might look to someone who had not known it as almost a part of the self, so, for the first time, he saw the primitive, vast, magnificent, barren, unkind simplicity of the mountain. As he said good-bye to it, he saw it turn into so much scenery, into the wonderful backcloth for an old country tale, tale of a child suckled by wolves, perhaps, or of wolves nursed by a woman.

Then he determinedly set his face towards the town and tramped onwards, into a different story.

"If I look back again," he thought with a last gasp of superstitious terror, "I shall turn into a pillar of salt."

I bite you in this writing on the thigh

the
perfect time
of quarter-
nips

tween
petalous
intervals
of
tit-
bud

I nibble you limb from limb
to limn your simmering

& heaven
is a morning
softly

gnawed, five
cats in idling
clowder

on the
bed, & you the
fifth &

yipping a
little yip, yawning
into a

caucus of
fur & purring
I don't

bite
right

Catnipped

Ira Wood

Sunday Angela returned home from a movie to find three male cats at her door and her own female, Natasha, pacing the windowsills. All night, Natasha pleaded with an urgency that cut into Angela like nothing since her own daughter's crying. Help me. Do something. Please do something. In a futile effort to sleep, she locked the cat in a bedroom downstairs with a plate of chunk light tuna fish but she could feel the animal's need, the feather tickling, the pulsing itch that could not be scratched. Had Natasha been the size of a tiger she would have mauled Angela before leaping into the streets to satisfy her hunger under a consenting moon. But she weighed seven pounds.

By mid-morning Monday Angela and her assistant, Michael, had already fought twice. "I can't stand this," he said, not unfamiliar with the torture of sexual longing. "Can't you get her fixed?"

"Too late, the vet said. I have to wait until she's out of heat."

Tuesday Michael called in sick. By then, her male cat, Boris, just six months old, had figured out what to do with his little pink dinkie, constantly erect now like the pop-up thermostat on a Perdue turkey. The two cats had to be separated at all times. Tuesday night every tom in the greater metropolitan area was at her door. They climbed the trees and leapt to the roof. They paced the gutters and sprayed the air conditioners. They hurled themselves at the windows. One shimmied through the old coal bin and clawed at the basement door from the inside. Her front porch smelled like the rest rooms at Burger King.

Wednesday she and Michael locked themselves in the darkroom all day and printed stills until her head was full of chemicals, her nostrils cement. When Corey, her ex-husband, arrived at her front door, she peered at him through burning eyes.

"I thought you invited me?" Disappointment clotted his voice.

Asphyxia made an honest woman of her. "I forgot."

He had come to have "the talk" she'd been avoiding since they had begun, guardedly, to laugh again; to face each other at parties and risk phone calls; to admit to more between them than Tina, the child he'd helped to raise.

Corey stared into his coffee cup for courage. Words were more difficult for him than theorems that ordered the physical world. "I don't feel guilty," he began tentatively, waiting for her resistance, a wall to bang his fist against.

She had never replaced Corey. The end of their marriage—his first, her second—was an empty room upon which she could close the door but never disconnect from her house. In the two years since they had separated, however, Angela had disappointed enough people to know that blame was only another way to hang on. It was the cat who had Angela's sympathy now, not this man who was just learning to speak, but poor Natasha, locked in solitary like an addict to suffer withdrawal alone. The sound of voices had only increased her plaintive wailing. Help me! Please, do something! "Corey, tell me something." Angela willed herself back to the conversation. "Are you happy?"

He didn't answer for a long time. "That I did what I had to do? Yes. I know the price was high. I know it was human lives."

"We broke up, Corey. This was not Vietnam." Angela began to pace. That long low moan, like the gurgle of a drowning man, was too much to take.

"Do you have a cat?"

She had never told him. She had accepted Natasha reluctantly. A cat represented failure to Angela, the lonely woman replacing love with a pet. She had been altogether surprised, however, by the passionate and intelligent creature with a capacity to love larger than any man she had ever known. "I was so busy I kept putting off getting her fixed."

"So *busy?* You don't think Tina going away to college this

year meant you couldn't bear to keep the cat from having more of her own?"

"Corey, you do not have my permission to have insight into my behavior."

"Why don't you do what my mom did?"

"Which was?"

"My dad wouldn't let her have any of the cats fixed."

"My father didn't either, but my mother did it anyway."

"My dad had a way of drinking the money that paid the vet's bills. You have a Q-tip?"

"Your mother did *that?*"

Corey was already in the bedroom when Angela joined him, hiding a Q-tip in her palm like a condom, embarrassed. Far from rejecting Corey, as Angela had feared, Natasha was in such discomfort that she welcomed the weight of his hand on her spine and offered up her butt as she had to everyone and everything including the vacuum cleaner. Her eyes asked Angela, Will *he* do something?

He had evidently watched his mother many times. It discomfited Angela to be reawakened to the sensual talents of a man it was easier to remember as cold. Corey massaged the cat at the nape of her neck. Angela had made herself forget the thick blond hair on his forearms, like wheat sprung out of rock. "Little One, trust me," he said. "Sweetheart, I won't hurt you." His voice was rich black coffee.

When he placed the Q-tip against the cat's vagina, swollen and sore, the size of the mouth on a Barbie Doll, the cat snapped her head back and tried to bite him. Corey eased the Q-tip in and out, in and out, giving it a little twist to the side when he was inside—like his style of fucking, she remembered, and caught herself blushing. The cat shrieked, dug her claws into the bed. Her rear end shook like a muscle gone into spasm, the howling increased to a murderous cry. And then all was quiet.

Angela was fascinated. "Shall we do it again?"

"She'll tell me if she wants to."

"Just next time," Angela said, "a little gentler. And talk to her more."

"Do you want to try?" he asked.

She and Corey lay full length on the bed. They were clothed, they still had their shoes on. They were not touching. But between them, and touching them both, was an ecstatic creature purring like an engine, paws in the air, rolling from side to side, satisfied for the first time in days. Again? Natasha asked with her huge green eyes. Are we going to do it again? What's next?

Remembering her old attraction to Corey was painful. An opening wide and deep within her, it belittled what she had felt for the men in her life since him. Those had been safe attractions, sweet ones, pleasures and pain she could handle. She had managed to believe that Corey and she herself had changed enough to neuter that once insatiable passion he had walked away from.

"She's telling us something," Corey said.

"Maybe not." She stroked the cat, who watched her expectantly and rose to her hand. "Maybe this is enough for one night." Angela was not yet ready to be touched that way again.

"Is it too late?"

When they had lived together, their chosen time to make love had always been early evening. Both of them found intense pleasure in their work. When the alarm rang in the morning they were already awake, eager to tackle the problems they had quit the day before. Early evening, however, was a garden of hungry night creatures and filtered light. In the early evening their minds began to slow as their senses quickened. They would collapse then, they would coil into one another, strum each other like guitars and emerge from their bed well tuned.

Angela wanted Corey. She wanted his honey vanilla skin.

She wanted the ripple of his laughter in her ear. She wanted his face drifting across her belly to her thighs, but even more she wanted to talk. To chew ideas as they had in the beginning. To face one another as hot active minds. To hack away at their problems with a common understanding as the prize. She had to try again.

"I won't ask you to forgive me," he said. "I can promise you that there is no one else. When there was it didn't last because I tried to turn her into you."

"Which me, Corey? You're not coming home to the woman you left."

"Am I coming home?"

It was her decision. He had done and said as much as he could. The rest was a risk she would have to take.

His eyes were wet when he buried his face in her neck. She raised one finger to his mouth to stop his kisses, then slid off her clothes and turned out the bedside lamp. Spreading her arms in invitation, she said, "This doesn't have to be wonderful after all this time."

"Be a lot easier if it was."

Corey had never been a timid lover but tonight she sensed him rating himself on a checklist. Should he kiss her breasts or hold them? Would she think he was rushing her if he cupped his palm hand around her mons? He did so and then drew it away.

"This is not working," Angela said, determined. She turned her back to him. Spoons, they used to call this position. "Touch me?" she said. His breath on the nape of her neck, his sex pressed against her bottom, his hand found the way to please her and discovered a memory of its own.

After she came, gently, she kissed his fingers. She mounted him as she had ten thousand times, too many years ago. "Remember?" she whispered.

Corey moved to a forgotten rhythm, a song he had once refused to hear. "It's coming back," he said.

"Corey don't let it go again?" Her eyes demanded this. "Keep it this time? Can we keep it?"

Corey shuddered and her life was at momentary peace. She laid her body against the length of his. Between her thigh and her forearm, Natasha found her place purring, confident and wise.

At Seventeen

Elizabeth
Alexander

I want to do it, want to snort and root
and forage in your skin and apertures.
It happens fast. It hits a frantic pitch.

I want to touch touch, suck suck, lick lick
like my kin in the animal kingdom.
Suction noises horrify and thrill me,

forensic evidence of what I'm doing
and doing and doing, pants around
my ankles, wigs in my hair. I am

sweaty and dirty, a little bit bloody,
smell of exactly what I have been
up to, sneak home like the criminal I am,

new memory like a seltzer in my crotch.

$\mathscr{S}$onnet

Elizabeth
Alexander

This morning I wished (once) to be a quiet
lover, but who can love with a closed mouth?
It opens, bites, is wet. The sounds come out.
Maybe it's how sounds release from corpses
when the undertaker turns them, last breath
sighing, free from will. In Mount Pleasant
I could hear elephants and tigers waking
each morning in the zoo, not copulating,
only trumpeting, roaring, announcing
their existence in indigenous tongues. These
noises I make are like dog whistles, air-raid
bells, touch-tones that tell the machine, play back
my messages, tell me who called, what they
said and who loves me, and why.

House Spirits

~

Stephen Minot

For Tony the morning has been the pits—the men taking off for the barn minutes after breakfast with no more than a grunt for her or the children, the weather turning dank and hot, the children surly, ready to detonate. Hanny, the nature lover, tried to save a wasp from a spider's web and was stung for her trouble. So much for altruism. Cliff, a sometime sexist at seven, hooted at his sister, and Tony couldn't help giving him more of a clout than he deserved. When quiet returned, she found that mice had tunneled into the bread she'd baked the previous night, crapping on what they couldn't eat.

That's all behind her now, but she can't flush the anger. Mind-pollution. It lingers, poisons everything. Old doubts bubble to the surface. Does being here make sense? Bad enough uprooting themselves from California and coming east to start again, but what if they guessed wrong? What if New Englanders hate good pottery? Here she is, thinking about money again, but how can she help it? What if they go broke a second time? What if some county sheriff decides he doesn't like the way they live and invites them to move again? Where this time? Meanwhile, she has to endure being trapped in this old kitchen, tending to kids like a farm-wife while the men convert the barn into a new studio. Does any of this make sense?

By lunch the poisons have begun to clear. She's almost human. Josh and Bojo come back. Relief in sight. But the moment they explode on the scene, she can see they're not part of the solution. They're in their vaudeville mood, stumbling around, cracking jokes, bellowing at each other, ears deadened by the saw, recounting the morning's disasters. Lanky Josh the straight man and big Bojo the clown with his walrus mustache, a comedy team that leaves her in the goddamned wings.

"How is it out in Marlboro land?" she says, trying to wedge herself between them. But she's speaking the wrong language. They thunder on, each claiming credit for slicing the electric cord with the Skillsaw, setting off a shower of glorious sparks all over the barn, damn near burning their future to the ground.

"Who-eee," from Bojo, his head embedded in the refrigerator, his big butt to the world, "we should do that every day."

"Gets the juices going," Josh says, voice bubbling under the spigot at the kitchen sink. "A 220-volt show."

Bojo finds a can of beer, flips it to Josh. "Comin' at you!" Can becomes basketball and snaps back to Bojo. "Hot potato!" The pace picks up, children join the game, shrieking, the dog barking, leaping, the can spinning, too fast for the eye to follow. Whang!—It hits the stove, blastoff in a plume of foam. It ricochets across the table, dishes shattering, strikes the wall, men and children whooping.

"Cut the shit!" Tony's voice kills them dead.

"Hey," Bojo says, "why so hostile?"

"Me? Hostile? Butch Cassidy and his pal drop in on their sweetie for a couple of laughs. I should be so lucky. Except the sweetie, as I remember it, didn't have kids, didn't keep house. The guys just kept her in the toy closet until they wanted to play."

Tableau: everyone staring at her.

"Hoo-boy, what's been going on?" Bojo says. "Sounds heavy."

"Better lay it out," Josh says. "This is coming on us from nowhere."

"Nowhere? Look around."

"Eyes and ears open," Josh says. "Let it flow."

"Too hot for group therapy. But things aren't right. Not since we moved into this creepy place."

"Give us a hint," Josh says. "What's not right that we don't already know about?"

"We may have been broke back on the Coast, but at least we were together. You know? We were potters together. Hell, I taught you. You two were a couple of dropouts working the crowd with junk jewelry. You didn't know a potter's wheel from a hubcap."

Bojo nods. "OK. And now we're taking over? Leaving you behind? It must be the house that's doing it. Old spirits hanging around in here." He winks at Cliff as if sharing a man-talk joke. "Old place like this lures us back into old ways. Ooo-ee-ooo." Cliff grins, but Hanny, younger, is wide-eyed. She's too smart to joke about spirits.

"Lay off the ghost stories. I'm trying to talk."

"Let her talk," Josh says. "Serious stuff going on."

"I don't want talk."

"You said you did."

"Don't tell me what I want."

"We're listening." Bojo puts a big hand to his ear, hard of hearing. Josh knocks it down.

"Easy, pal. Easy."

There's a silence.

"OK, guys, I don't like divisions. I don't like assignments. I'm a country girl that didn't like what they were doing to my mother or my sisters. I didn't run away to end up like them."

"I hear you now," Bojo says. "A cry for help. Cavalry to the rescue."

Josh picks up the bugle call. "Tonight we take over the kitchen."

The two of them hug her at the same time, nuzzling her. At first she shakes her head, smiling but trying to push them off. They still don't have it right. Not at all. She doesn't want to be queen for a day. But she's too tired to bring them up short a second time. Besides, with their arms around her and hers around them for the first time in a long time it isn't quite so bad.

A reformation of sorts begins: Bojo mops beer from walls and floor, Josh makes sandwiches for everyone, the kids help. They eat at the table, muted, staying in place. The men wash the dishes and take turns looking after the kids while Tony goes down to the barn and cuts planks for work tables. She's OK with tools, always has been. In school she talked her way into shop courses, the only girl among boys, until teachers, parents, everyone put a stop to it. Her hands, arms remain strong. Not until they moved here did they start to separate—men in the barn, women and children in the house. Perhaps Bojo wasn't kidding about the old place taking hold of them; maybe it really is driving them into deadening work, converting them to old ways, sucking their spirits dry. She shudders, sensing generations of dour old folk lurking in the walls, embedded in the dry plaster, whispering, whispering.

But now the whine of the Skillsaw silences them, drives them back. Her mood begins to float. Even when the barn takes on the afternoon heat, she remains light—bone tired and soaked with sweat, but light. A new studio is taking shape and she is once again a part of it.

She realizes how much she has missed the ooze of clay, the sweet-talk of the wheel, the anticipation, not knowing what shape will evolve until her hands show her. It has been months since they dismantled the old studio, pulled out, headed east. Just when she was beginning to grind clam shells from Pismo Beach, adding it to her grog, creating new textures, devising new glazes. A terrible wrench, suspending all that, selling their equipment— the old kiln, their stock of clay, their two treadle wheels. Terrible but necessary. A conspiracy of bank and sheriff at their backs. A cheap, dirt cheap abandoned farm ahead.

A bargain, all right, sight unseen; but there is something forbidding about the house. It is weighed down with old, earnest effort, deep faith, past failures. So old. So many layers. Framed photos of farm folk still hang on the wall—faces glum, names forgotten. How long, Tony wonders, before the three of them will really take possession?

She consoles herself with the promise that with new loans they will start over. Josh, the money man, has figured dollars and cents. Abandoned farmland in Maine is a bargain compared with

California, and this gives them something to work with—a studio with real space, an electric wheel, a hotter kiln, a chance to do stoneware. Josh has worked it all out. The facts are solid, encouraging. But the spirit of the place—that's another thing.

At the end of the day her muscles hum and her mood stays high. Bojo proposes a young-people's party and then a late dinner for grownups.

"Party?" Cliff asks. "Whose birthday?"

"Yours," Josh says.

"No it isn't."

"Every day is if you keep your eyes open."

"You stole that from Tony."

"Public property. Come on, want to learn how to make a quickie sponge cake?"

Bojo and Hanny make up a children's meal of chicken patties and vegetables while Tony, relieved of kitchen duties, picks out tapes, fills the air with music. She and the men drink wine, the kids limeade, they throw darts at a pockmarked target, singing along with Joni Mitchell, eat when they feel like it, feeding sponge cake to Jose the dog. Wine and limeade are spilled, paper is folded into darts, the goat is brought in to enjoy the scene and finish the scraps. They've broken the spell of too much work, too much worry, begun to recapture the spirit they almost lost. But the party, Tony realizes, is only just beginning.

When the kids' chapter comes to a close, it's hard for them to let go. Josh and Bojo work on the decompression, reading from Edwin Lear, selecting the story about the children who go around the world in a blue boat with green spots. The storybook children are all well known, all personal friends. The pleasure for Hanny and Cliff depends not on surprise but anticipation. The reading is ritual. The responses, slightly different each time, are part of that ritual. As always, Hanny puts up a fuss when the Pussy-Cat and the Quangle-Wangle bite off the tail feathers of the sixty-five parrots. "It's so mean." As always, Cliff tells Hanny that the parrots like it, they like the attention. Where did he pick that up?

After the reading Bojo tells them a story about Otto the Octopus who flunked out of Berkeley and sells Korean jewelry to tourists down on Fisherman's Wharf. Otto is also well known to them all, but the ways in which he employs his eight arms to greet the tourists and occasionally lift their wallets, car keys, and wristwatches, and the ways he sweet-talks the police and judges into granting him freedom vary every night.

It is almost ten before the children are asleep, the goat is put back in its shed, and the house is populated only by adults. The three of them are now as they were their first years together, as they still were from time to time after the children appeared. Since moving into this old place, though, they have worked all day, eaten with the children, and turned in early, bone weary as pioneers. Now, at last, they are allowing themselves old indulgences.

Without plan or discussion all three of them change out of their sweaty Levi's. Tony puts on a long skirt and blouse. Josh wears white pants and a blue sports shirt. Bojo finds clean khakis somewhere and a maroon shirt. "New skin," Tony calls it. They all have new skin.

Salad making is a rite of improvisation—lettuce leaves from their own garden, cheese and beans from the market, bleeding tomatoes, palm oil. Hands move, adding a harmony of seasoning; fingers dip; lips taste. The men make a mock soufflé, and Tony salvages bread from the tunneled loaves, dusting off turds, heating slices with garlic butter.

They eat in a gentle blur of wine, candlelight, and laughter. The air is moist and warm, bringing beads of sweat to their brows. If there are old spirits lurking in the walls, they are kept at bay.

The eating over, Bojo pours sweet apple brandy into a small

glass, dips a finger in, and extends it to Tony. She licks it leisurely. Josh offers her the same. Then it is her turn, holding out a moist finger first to one of them and then to the other in turn. They lick lips and sigh.

Josh rolls a joint and the incense fills the room. They remain at the table, hands touching from time to time. When there is conversation, it springs from nowhere, moves without direction, erratic as a butterfly. Bojo brings out his guitar, blows the dust off, and sings Irish folk songs. Amazing, Tony thinks, that someone so solid, so bulky, should have such light fingers.

Time wafts away. They are cut loose from days on either side. The past recedes into dark corners, the future remains unborn. Dirty dishes vanish along with debts, fears, resentments, plans. The three of them float in a blue boat with green spots, a sea without horizons. They listen to crickets and unknown creatures that buzz and click.

"All those love calls," Josh says. "They're trying to find each other."

"We're ahead of them," Bojo says.

A long, contented silence. A sigh or two.

"Sixty-three parrot feathers," Bojo says, shaking his head. "Beau-ti-ful."

"Sixty-five," Josh murmurs.

"Beau-ti-fuller," Tony says.

Tony feels her skin glowing, feels droplets of sweat trickle. The men, gently lit with candlelight, become dream figures— Josh a lean castaway, Bojo, no longer a clown, a trainer of circus bears. His maroon shirt is open to the waist and draws her hand to his chest, a warm barrel. A furry barrel. His moist hair, glistening, smells faintly saline. She looks first at one man and then at the other, feeding on them, tasting them. Anticipation hangs in the air, drawn taut.

She smiles, sighs, and languidly removes her jersey. She has worn no underthings. To be topless with a long, formal skirt and bare feet is a state she enjoys almost as much as nudity.

She can feel two needs in her now—one to delay, to hold off as long as possible, to savor, to sustain that great, verdant, open space; the other to rush it, to hear the rip of fabric and the slap of bodies. How fortunate, she thinks, to have some of each, to enjoy the tug. How lovely to have them back once again, together once again.

Bojo takes another toke, stands, and, stumbling just a bit, moves behind her and begins massaging her neck. Those guitar-playing fingers know instinctively which muscles are knotted, how to release them strand by strand until there is no resistance.

A creak on the stairs. They turn and see Hanny standing there, halfway down, her nuzzling blanket held to her lips.

"Have to go pee," she says softly, only half awake. Normally she goes on her own, but she is confused by sleep.

"How about a lift?" Tony says.

She goes up to Hanny and carries her down the stairs and into the bathroom, the girl's head gratefully resting against a familiar breast. Tony sets the girl on the toilet and waits. Then she tears off paper for her. Hanny's body seems sculptured, as beautiful now as it will be, in other ways, years from now.

"Anything else?" Tony asks.

"Uh uh."

Tony takes her hand and passes through the dining room. The two men are at the table; the candle stubs still burn; the sweet-grass smell hangs in the breathless night air. In the absence of time, there is nothing to interrupt.

Tony climbs the stairs, her bare feet silent, her long skirt rustling softly, and puts Hanny into her bed. As she bends over to kiss her, Hanny reaches up and touches her mother's bare breast, smiles, then closes her eyes. The smile lingers.

On the way back down the stairs, Tony passes two sepia portraits hanging on the wall. Each in a separate frame, the husband is set slightly higher, then the wife. Neither smiles. They stare at her in the candlelight, and for just a moment she feels something drain from her. But then she glides down toward her men, her spirit regained.

Back at the table she sips wine, eats a crust of bread. Josh takes the guitar and picks out the melody from some Telemann piece, plucking one string at a time. It sounds to Tony like a harp.

Later—minutes or perhaps hours—they head to their bedroom on the first floor, the one with the spool bed. There is a bar of moonlight across the spread. On the way, Tony lets her skirt drop to the floor without pausing. It is her last article of clothing. The men are still fully dressed.

She lies on the bed, one knee raised and one hand on her stomach, moonbathing. While watching the men sliding out of their skins once again, it occurs to her that while it is always different with infinite varieties depending on moods and needs, there is a kind of recurring pattern, an honored ritual. Bojo always begins. Always. And he is never interrupted until he is through. His style is strong, demanding, loud. Hard rock. There is a thundering rush to it, almost too fast. Josh, close beside them, will hold back, will take pleasure in anticipation. From time to time he will caress with hand or lips, but he will make no major move until the end of the first performance. He will wait until she is calm and breathing evenly again. Then he will begin, hands gliding, and soon their bodies will slide together, moist as wet clay. He will work himself up more gradually, more subtly. When he finally peaks, it will be her third or fourth that night. Exhausted, she will slip almost at once into sleep, dreaming, perhaps, of one complex and loving man, part impulsive, and part deliciously deliberate.

Such intense feelings, she realizes, have substance, staying power. They will permeate these old walls, dwell there as spirits, will speak to future residents. She smiles, knowing that at last-they have begun to take possession of the house.

Selected Orgasms

Selected Orgasms

Nin Andrews

The Orgasm's First Date:
On their first date, Franz asked Maria: When was the last time you had an orgasm? Maria stared back at him with the wan look of orgasm starvation.

The Hypothetical Orgasm:
Franz looked at the orgasm from afar. Maria thought about it. The two analyzed it, as if it were a hypothesis. All at once they were seized by the orgasm. For a moment they looked back at the world as one looks at a hypothetical world.

Cézanne's Orgasm:
Beneath the brushstrokes the orgasms became peaches and pears. Such golden reds and oranges!

Van Gogh's Orgasm:
The orgasm flies through the air, its hair flaming out across the night.

Pollock's Orgasm:
Maria sighed, if only he'd learn a little self-control. . . .

Picasso's Orgasm:
She knew what he was thinking. How he'd like to strip off her white skirt and silk blouse and panties and take her apart piece by piece. See how she works. And leave her spread all over the playroom floor.

De Kooning's Orgasm:
It seemed to rise into the room without them.

Cézanne's Second Orgasm:
Sometimes the orgasm dreams it's a peach. It basks in the sun and summer rain. And ripens in its own sweet time.

De Kooning's Second Orgasm:
When the orgasm is not a part of the man, the woman and the dream, it cools. Then they call it an abstract orgasm.

The Monogamous Orgasms:
Maria was one woman with three orgasms. In each orgasm she was another woman. In each orgasm she saw another man though she slept with only one man.

The Bouquet of Orgasms:
A bouquet of orgasms rested on the bedside table. They admired the recently spritzed petals. All too quickly they drifted away: Franz, Maria, and the orgasm.

The Absent Orgasm:
Franz and Maria don't have to be in every single panel. Sometimes orgasms take place without them.

The Statue's Orgasm:
The orgasm is a cloud imprisoned in the stone flesh. For centuries it has been moaning silently.

The Lousy Orgasm:
Afterwards they ate calamari that tasted like tiny tires.

The Old Orgasm:
Orgasms arrived weeks ago and were filled with sky. In the beginning Maria thought they were holy, and she collected them, folding them neatly into dresser drawers. But little did she know. Orgasms don't keep. After a while the orgasms became nothing but humid, city air. Often she fell asleep listening to the soft meow of summer nights. What disconcerted her was the ambulance in the distance, calling her name.

The Winter Orgasm:
Seduction is the sound of snow falling inside their skin in ecstasy. Exhaling plumes of fog, Franz and Maria slowly froze into an icy silence.

A Green Orgasm:
Sometimes, on a windless summer day, even the leaves are quivering.

The Orgasm's Promise:
"If you make love to me this once," Maria sighed, "I'll keep your orgasm forever. And treasure it like a tiny diamond."

The Anonymous Orgasm:
The orgasm is always anonymous. Still they tried to remember whose name to call.

The Orgasms of Things:
Maria didn't like to be left alone at night. She said the house made strange noises and kept her awake.

The Anti-Orgasms:
The tears we can't cry, the orgasms we can't have. We enjoy them, too, all that we can.

The Zen of the Orgasm:
You must enjoy leaving the orgasm as much as entering it. That is the way of the enlightened.

The Orgasm's Mantra:
The orgasm is always whispering one word in Franz and Maria's ears: "Good-bye."

Fiddle Trees

Samuel Green

Hiking back late from a dance,
full moon brushing the shoulder
of the ridge, new snow
light on the ground, we pause
along the trail to listen
at the sound two close-grown cedars make
rubbing in a random breath of air.
Fiddle trees
my grandfather called them.

How long do we stand there? Enough
to take that music
into our own limbs for the quick walk
home, the long night's steady hum.

You Ask Me About Birds and I Tell You

Samuel Green

If sometimes, when a heron
spread her great wings to dry
in whatever sun there was I
thought of you, the hidden strength
unfolding from your body,

and if, watching hawks work
through air so still only the sunlit tips
of their wings moved, like fingers,
I remembered the tips of your fingers
in their slow love circles, oh

yes, and if I've noticed
how a raven's wings luff
overhead like spilled breath,
how an owl's scoop air without sound
in its quickest flight,

it was to understand this,
our coming together, the way
pine siskins leave a tree, suddenly, all
at once, and between their startled wings
those drunken patches of light.

The Star of China

Christopher Noel

Mrs. Strong looked out across the field as she pounded the turkey legs over her porch railing. She set her eyes on the far tree-line that crossed, like a boundary drawn strangely through the sky, over the very end of her world. It kept the family in. Though the line was far away and stretched through the sky, still it made her feel safe. She felt she was living on a smaller earth, provided for her and hers. She hit another leg sharply against the wood.

To her left stood the Turkey House, long and narrow like a box, with a sloping silver roof and many small windows. The turkeys let out a constant uneasy babble, as if they were certain their days were numbered. And they were ab-so-*lute*-ly cor-*rect*, thought Mrs. Strong, splitting the next one at its joint into fleshy upper thigh and scaly, useless ankles. By the end of the afternoon she would have a basketful of the sticklike lower legs with their claws clenched shut.

One of Mrs. Strong's greatest pleasures had been the naming of her children, and she glowed to think of the day when Raphael Strong would take a wife and paint his name up on the side of the Turkey House, beside his father's.

The real reason she had chosen the names she had was that perhaps they would work to attract mysterious lovers from far away. Then, the best of the outside world, what was most new and exciting, could come to her and she would never have to leave here.

The wind blew and there was a murmur in the tall grass throughout the expanse of her smaller earth. She thought she felt it rock a bit, and then, looking out again to the tree-line, pulled tight and even before limitless space, she found she could relax and lean back with a deep breath, closing her hands over the arms of her wooden chair. She thought vaguely of the turkey claws and wondered, smiling, if her arms and legs didn't look like sticks too when she was seen from a distance.

Mrs. Strong was a large woman with a broad face marked by nut-brown lines that traveled across her forehead and others that came up from her chin and went into the middle of her cheeks, lines that were usually almost invisible, but then took charge of her face when she would smile, making her appear to be the most satisfied person in the world.

She was smiling now because her daughter, Jessamine, had just come into view way out in the field. She could see the slim, young figure running like a slip of shadow against the sky, along the rim of the world. This sight was not, for her, a symbol of their life together. Though the girl was distant by nature, and Mrs. Strong knew this, her idea of her was different, was of her daughter sitting beside her on the porch. Often they would stay here together without speaking, looking out at the great field and the sky that stood up for them like the future. Words would have spoiled it.

But what Mrs. Strong *would* have told Jessamine was all about love. She would have told her how to make herself look as if love were coming near, with red strokes across the cheeks and a faraway cast in the eye. When a young woman has that color in her cheeks and that cast in her eyes it is as if, in any month of the year, the season to follow has reached her already. While everyone stands in winter, she has warmth lighting her and knows just which horizon to face to catch sight of the green tint beginning to spiral out from that one tree or low ridge in the field. And in the flush of spring, while others are joyous, tasting the sweet air on the run, she becomes quiet and walks with long strides and the calm face of one who knows that summer, a mile away or perhaps two, will be tall and heavy, drawing his hot feet through the field and turning them brown. And no, when summertime did come through, you could not run, if you were this special girl. You would be surefooted and sober, looking from side to side, bracing for the winds of autumn. Summertime means you stay put, and you grow up, thought Mrs. Strong, sitting still, eyes shut in the warm sun. "HOOO!" she called out. "HOOO! HOOOOOO!"

Because it was a hot summer day and Jessamine was sprinting, her forehead was soaked and her short blond hair damp in the bangs. Her dress clung to her wet legs as she ran. She had come clear across the upper field now and could see her mother, at an angle, far off on the porch of the small house, looking old, whining like a baby.

She stopped running but didn't walk home. She pushed the wet hair out of her face and listened for the sound of the brook which ran through this field and into the forest. Jessamine knew right where it was, but she liked to listen for it and pretend every time to discover it. She skirted the field until she reached a place where the trees parted, and here she came upon a little brook that made a very sweet sound as it entered the woods. She found a flat rock, too, by the water, that was covered with moss, sat down on it, and crossed her legs. She crossed her arms too and put a calm look into her eyes.

She tried to let the sound of the water flow into her soul and the cooler wind here pass right through her. In a book about China, she had read that people in that country sit on the edges of rivers, lakes, and ponds, and calm themselves all the way, until nature drifts into them whole.

Jessamine had always found this to be impossible. But she knew what she would do. She would bring the King of China himself to this rock, and let *him* sit down. She was sure that the people who ran the fair and took care of the King had never read that book about China, so they'd never let him sit alone by water. More than anything else in this world, Jessamine wanted to do something wonderful for someone all her own. Her mother had told her that this was the greatest pleasure on earth, and Jessamine believed it. She used to have a cat, but it had died last winter. And anyway, nothing she did for it seemed to hit the spot; no, it had to be exactly what the someone who was all yours had wanted for a very long time.

꒰

The next morning, the Strongs left the house and walked the two-and-a-half miles to town, Mrs. Strong and Jessamine out front, pressing ahead, Agee and Raphael lagging. But Raphael was only lagging to be like his father. He couldn't help admiring his sister, in her short red-and-yellow-striped dress, and the two bright spots, just pinpricks from this distance, moving up and down where the sun hit the skin of her calves.

The Strongs smelled popcorn and the hot cherry candy which, Jessamine knew, was swirled with big wooden spoons, like boat paddles, in a copper pot over a fire. Apples stuck on long sticks were dipped into the candy and then they cooled hard as glass. They passed under a white cloth banner that had the word "FAIRGROUNDS" painted on it in blue.

"I want to ride the giraffe!" yelled Raphael, now breaking from his father's side and pointing out ahead, laughing in a loud shallow way as he ran toward the circular fence of barn-red posts. A chain ran from a stake at the center to the animal's leg, where it joined a rusted cuff. The giraffe was nearly six feet tall. It had a matted, steel-colored mane and a lower lip that drooped.

"Sit atop Omar, Tower of the Jungle!" a man shouted from the top of a barrel by the fence. "Yes, from on top of this magnificent beast, why *you* can see all that *he* can see!"

Raphael gave the man the money and was lifted onto Omar's back. The giraffe kicked a little and then stood still, eyes serene and staring into space. The boy clung to the neck, looked as far as he could, and soon recognized the new tin roof of Carl Butts's sawmill shining in the sun across the street.

Agee stood at the fence, watching his son and swatting mosquitoes. Jessamine tugged at her mother's arm.

"Do you suppose it will still be there?" Mrs. Strong asked.

Jessamine hopped twice. "What? Of *course* he'll be there. What do you mean? The King has been living for *one hundred years*. Of course."

They passed by a man riding backwards on a bull. He kicked his legs out and threw up his arms, yelling, "Wooo!" Mrs.

Strong looked down at Jessamine and smiled. Several men watching the rider also yelled, "Wooo!"

They soon reached a tent shaped like the Turkey House. It was divided into sections and covered in front by white canvas with slits cut in it for going in and out. Each section had pictures painted on it for what was inside, and big, three-dimensional-looking letters over the top. Outside, men stood on top of barrels and each excitedly told about his attraction. People paid money and slipped inside.

Mrs. Strong and Jessamine passed by several who told about trained snakes, and dogs that were crossed with sheep and looked "like the cutest little lambs that bark and howl too!" One man with a wedge-shaped beard and a tilted smile called out, "*There* you go, ma'am, and wouldn't the little lady like to dip her hand in the sea of oysters and pick the one with the pearl inside?" Last year, Jessamine had tried this. The "sea" was an old bathtub and the oyster she chose had had nothing but black water inside that ran all over her hands when she opened it.

At last, they stopped in front of the largest section of the tent. The letters on the canvas were red and tinted with gold all around: YO QUANG—WISE KING OF CHINA. There was a picture of a silver gong with wavy lines coming from it, and another of a light-blue star hanging low over a range of dark mountains. The ticket man on the barrel was the same one who had been there for the last three years, the one who reminded Jessamine of her father. Both men were skinny, but this one wore a silly red T-shirt with YO QUANG painted on the front. His arms moved wildly as he talked and his face, which was small and paler than her father's, shortened and lengthened in a grimace.

"That's right," he began as the two looked up at him. He got a faraway look in his eyes, like he was in love. "This man is wise through and through. He knows it all, *that* you can believe . . ." Jessamine mouthed the words right along with him.

"Taken by thieves he was from the throne of China *fifty*

years ago and sailed 'cross the ocean and 'round the world. Wisdom, *wisdom* he's got from all he's been through. And then he came to our land to *educate* us Americans. We freed him from the thieves, that's the truth, and now he's doing us a turn. And we should feel lucky, *lucky*. Think of the poor folks off in China right now on their hands and knees with no king. But here, we've built him a throne and he's with us, with *us*. Oh, he's gonna go back, all the way back around the world one of these fine days, soon now. But while he's with us here, he's happy to help. Happy! Though never foolish, like we are when we get happy. Not a foolish bone. Just look at him. Folks, this man is wise *through* and *through!*" The man pulled a cloth out of his pocket and wiped his face with it.

"Then if he's so smart," said a boy now coming out of the slit in the tent, "why don't he answer any questions if I ask?" His eyes were sharp.

"It's easy, son. You just don't ask the *right* questions. Remember, YO QUANG has heard it all and knows the answers complete. He's tired of the same old ones. Now you think of some new ones. You sit right down and *think*, or the King'll start packing up for home."

The boy nodded and popped back inside. Mrs. Strong and Jessamine followed him after paying the announcer. Inside, it was dimly lit. As they moved forward through the weak yellow light, their feet shuffled through a layer of thin, dry leaves, larger and shaped differently from any Jessamine had seen on trees around here. Ever since last summer she had had one taped to the upper left corner of the full-length mirror in her room. The canvas ceiling hung down in several places with the weight of the wooden lanterns that had candles burning inside them. The walls were covered with long sheets of purple paper with chalky white designs and faces drawn in rows.

Three other people stood up ahead, in front of a rope that stretched across the whole room. On the right side was an old man, stooped beside a much younger woman whose arm was linked through his. They kept shifting their feet and whispering back and forth. Toward the left was a tall motionless man with a broad back. The boy who had come outside sat over to the right by the tent wall, covering his legs entirely with the strange leaves. There was a very sweet scent in the air that came from two torches stationed one on each side of the King's throne, and two thick lines of smoke rose and dissolved at the ceiling.

Mrs. Strong and Jessamine drew up to the rope, trying to breathe without disturbing the King's air. The throne stood about ten feet away, and was maybe five feet high, draped over with a long robe of light-blue silk that fell all the way from the King's shoulders to the dark dust of the floor. His round head stuck through this robe so that it looked like a ball balancing there. He leaned against the throne's back and stared straight ahead without blinking. On top of his head was a dark purple hat, like a squat triangle, with a white star glowing dimly on it. His face was broad and his eyes were large and black. His gaze was fixed along a line that passed over the heads of the viewers and out through the slit and then on, Jessamine thought, over the plains to the horizon.

For her part, Mrs. Strong was wondering if this man really *could* speak or hear anything. He had never even moved his eyes around, so far as she knew, during all his time at the fair, and he only blinked once when a child threw a bottle against the legs of the throne, two summers ago. She looked where the robe came down over his shoulders and tried to imagine how his body was underneath. The shoulders were very narrow and it seemed that the body must be puny and ridiculous. She wondered about the legs, hanging down under all the fine fabric. How much did they resemble the legs of a turkey?

"Um, sir? Do you want to leave for China right away? Are you ready to go now?" Jessamine's voice was soft, as if she expected the King to spring off his throne at such a question. Instead, he kept staring out the slit. She whispered sideways, "Did he move his mouth? Did he move his mouth a *little?*"

Mrs. Strong squinted through the gloom to consider the face. The skin was certainly *not* smooth like the polished surface of an oriental figurine, the one Agee had brought her back from San Francisco. No, it was leathery and the cheeks were pocked and puffy. The eyes, though, were deep and beautiful. Then, she noticed that even they were surrounded by loose and puckered skin.

A woman drawing a small child by the hand burst into the room. "Just look at him, Wendy! Look at the eyes," she said, leaning down toward her girl and drawing the word "eyes" out in a loud whisper. "Just think what he could tell us if we could get him to trust us, if we could take him home." The woman straightened her back and stared at the King with her hands on her hips. She shook her head slowly. "To *see* those proud eyes go around in our house, studying our *things*, to see that old sour puss break into a grin!" The woman herself grinned now up at the King, who stared out of the tent until his vision reached the first fields of China.

On the way home, Raphael and Mr. Strong told about the man who had let a ball of fire roll down his arms and about the woman who had danced so well on a block of ice that smoke had risen up around her. Jessamine laughed that they had been tricked blind, and they laughed and pushed her back and forth between them as they all walked up the dusty dirt road.

Mrs. Strong was quiet, behind them, walking steadily, eyes toward home. She was unable to forget the round head with the deep eyes. She had a vision in which these eyes stopped staring into space and bent down until they were looking right at her. Then the grin that that woman had wanted to see came over his face and he began to laugh long and like thunder as the two torches slowly went out.

Retracing her way to town through the darkness much later, Jessamine shivered, even in sweater and pants. A quarter moon kept pace above her right shoulder, her shoes made short sliding noises, and even though nobody was near her, she knew that someone was listening to her footsteps coming for him.

In a few minutes, Jessamine slipped quietly into the tent and bent down under the rope at the front of the room. After seven steps, she reached her right hand up, and felt the empty seat covered with smooth cloth, moved around to the back of the throne and felt down along the tent wall. Her hand fell on a solid surface that ran beside her like the edge of a wooden box. She reached into it. No hand closed around hers weakly but she found the wrist. She pulled her hand back out and then centered it on the King's body, picked him up in her arms and held him against her.

He was little, not much larger than the turkeys she had carried, limp and still warm, from where their heads had been chopped off. She took a blanket out of the box and wrapped him up in it. He didn't have any legs at all and his hands were quite large. His body was pillow-shaped and his head, with its short bristly hair, felt hard and rough against the skin of her neck. His arms encircled her shoulders. She heard him breathing softly by her ear and she gave him a little kiss above his ear, where he tasted like the smell of the torches by his throne.

She left the tent and the fairground, seeing no one but Omar, standing dark in the quarter-moonlight, watching her? No, sleeping, his head didn't move as she passed by.

Though he was tightly wrapped in the blanket, the King often twitched and squeezed around her as they took the road out of town; she worried he would catch a cold. Once, he lifted his head and looked out over the dark fields. She heard him breathe inward suddenly and recognized the small suction sound of his mouth opening. Jessamine petted his head back down onto her shoulder and stroked his back. She felt his heart beating faster than before and she knew exactly why.

"In China right now," she assured him in a whisper, "it is getting bright out. The birds are just beginning and only you would understand what they are saying. The flowers are putting their faces out, and they look just like you, don't they, with your face so round. Yes, in China, my only, there is a houseboat for us, and it's moving through a garden."

Jessamine brought the King up into the loft of the Turkey House where she had prepared a nest for him out of old feathers. Underneath the birds half woke up, then quieted again. She tucked the blanket all around him in the nest, then stayed with him for a while, leaning over with her face next to his. She could not see his eyes, but she changed her breathing so that it was shallow and quick, matching his.

The next day, she decided to change his name to Daisy because he smelled so sweet. She could tell that he liked his new name. He gazed up at her from his nest, inside a warm rectangle of sunlight, so she lowered his dirty maroon blanket as far as she dared. His head and body looked so much like two lumps of mud stuck together that she wondered how he could have lasted; when she sniffed his belly, he even had the bright smell of mud. His arms were long slender branches, peeled but lumpy and snapped at the elbow, and his hands, palms-down on his chest, were the jumbo doughy pancakes that you pour carefully to make fingers in the pan. She covered him up again.

Except to shiver, Daisy never moved, even when she stepped back and forth in front of him, telling him every little thing on her mind. He stared straight across the room, through a little window, at the sky, taking breaths that seemed more like imitations of breathing. What he was doing was letting nature drift into him, preparing himself for the flat rock by the brook and for all that was coming.

Mrs. Strong sat in her front porch chair, gazing over her own smaller earth. The tree-line, always dependable, hung at the end, but it was being crossed by a quickly invading thunderstorm. In her hands, she held the body of a turkey that needed plucking. She gripped it firmly around the middle and tried to recall what it felt like to be passionately in love. She remembered running through field after field in an early-summer storm like this one, with her brand-new husband Agee, almost twenty years ago.

Jessamine sat in front of her at the edge of the porch, facing out into the wind, refusing to carry one more bird from where they had been beheaded by Agee and Raphael, on the other side of the Turkey House. Yes, she was in one of her moods now, though just this morning she had been a regular chatterbox, asking how to catch someone's eye. Mrs. Strong had leaned back and said, "You mean a boy's?" Jessamine had said, "Kind of." Mrs. Strong laughed at the bashfulness, but not too hard. She put on a serious expression and for good measure added that this was a very serious matter. She knew that Jessamine had been walking into town a lot lately, coming home with odd groceries like Vienna Sausages, cabbage, watercress, and frozen Chinese dinners, things the girl would never select for herself. And she'd lately noticed the calmness and flush in her daughter's face, and that faraway cast in her eyes. Mrs. Strong suspected that the boy in question was none other than Sam Akers, the store owner's thin but well-spoken son. So she told her daughter to try every means available. She said that a person can't just walk around expecting the world to take notice. She told her daughter to think what it was the boy most wanted to hear, or what it was he most wanted a girl to be, and then say it, and be it, over and over, until either he comes around or tells you he's not interested. "All this in-between nonsense," she had said, "is only fit for our turkeys, who can't decide a solitary thing in their entire lives."

The girl had paid complete attention, even went and changed into her prettiest pink-and-green dress, which she was still wearing, and Mrs. Strong rejoiced at being able to teach from experience.

Just now, a headless turkey ran around the corner of the Turkey House and crossed before them at an angle, but Jessamine's head didn't move to follow the path of the hearty runner; she seemed instead to be staring at the near wall of the Turkey House, with its one small window up high. After an interesting series of senseless decisions, the bird lay down at last, almost gingerly, beside a gray stepladder, glugging blood into the dust.

Mrs. Strong laughed loudly, then a flare occurred in the sky, like the sun catching the edge of a diamond, followed by the long gravelly booming. "Isn't it going to be a good one?" she called out to her daughter's back. She meant that Jessamine's *life* was going to be a good one, not only the storm. She took in the heavy, smoky smell storms have and she felt the urge to lead her girl out into the field beneath all that glory, to soak in all the world had to offer.

Tossing the body of the turkey from one elbow-cleft to the other in a low arc, she yelled, "A big one!" Another brief diamond-flare took its unexplainable shape just above them, and it struck Mrs. Strong that she was happier now than she had ever been, and she was about to scream it out into the suddenly commanding rain when she saw Jessamine rise and push off the edge of the porch, her dress snatched and filled by the wind. Even from behind, she could see that she had turned into a beautiful woman. She thought this was an absolute miracle, and she called out, "Ab-so-*lute mir*-acle!" after this grace, disappearing into the busy air.

Jessamine sat across from Daisy beneath the little window, smiling shyly, drenched, leaning back with her hands out behind her so that her straight arms completed a triangle with her back and the wooden floor. Her legs, crossed at the ankles, pointed toward the nest. The leg on the bottom bounced regularly up and down, so that she kept feeling the rough board with the back of her knee.

"Want a cola?"

Daisy lay, tilted half upright in the nest, blanket snug under his chin, even his arms safe and warm, and he stared straight at her. All around him were boxes and cans of food he wouldn't eat, not even from her own hand. He couldn't help but look at her anymore: her eyes, the shine of her shoulders. Giving in, she crawled over and lay beside him.

He breathed through his mouth and from down deep came a thin whistle. This was his way of singing to her, but how thin it was compared to the thunder outside almost broke her heart.

She slowly turned her head toward his, but he kept his eyes forward, being difficult. She smiled. "You think I'm sweet, Daisy, don't you? You think I'm about the sweetest thing you've seen." She spoke into his ear, pressed her thumb into the surprising pink flap of his earlobe. Through the window across the room flew the fine spray of rough waters. She and Daisy lay on the broad deck of a houseboat, rain striking the firm bamboo roof. They could feel the river forming under them, ready to pick them up and move them off with that first gigantic scrape, that bulky graceful slide. "You're taking me back with you," she said.

She sat up, moved in front of him, loosened the shoulder straps of her dress, and brought the pink cloth slowly down. He looked at her loyally, without blinking. She took hold of his hand and placed it on her shoulder, then slid it over the curve and down to the elbow.

"I've got something to show you," she whispered. Daisy tightened his hand around her arm. She lowered the dress over more shiny, damp skin. "Look," she said. "Here. Can you see? I've been waiting forever to show you. I've had it since I was born." She pointed to where the skin was even lighter than the rest, where, near the center of her chest, there was a pearl-colored circle. She craned her neck so she could see it too, just barely. Well, not a perfect circle. "That's right," she told him. Luminous, it was, in the twilight of the room. "You're right, it's the Star of China."

In the Restrooms of Europe

Tom Whalen

In the dirty restrooms of the European metropolises I saw men and men, and men and women, and women and women making love. Some, in fact, weren't actually making love, but they were thinking of making love, and for a moment I too wanted to make love, there, in the dirty bathrooms of the European metropolises. We call this condition, for lack of a better word, loneliness, though I for one wasn't lonely, more intellectually (I'm not, by the way, what anyone by any stretch of the etc. would call an intellectual) curious, though I might have been, on second thought, a little lonely, might have been feeling a bit that, a bit sexually deprived, in need of physical contact, there in the pissoirs and WCs of Europe. Yes, I might have felt an urge, a need, desire, whatever, mania, oestrus, passion, yen, zeal, appetite, avarice, nympholepsy for my flesh to smack as only flesh can against the flesh of another, it's true, there, in the waning light of a Parisian afternoon, or a Bieler morning, or a Viennese noon, to put my hand or chest or kneecaps or sexual organ on the flesh of someone who at that moment wanted also to put his etc. on someone's etc. There, in the toilets of Europe, whether graced or not with attendants, people went about their business which included making love. Or, again, if not actually making love, at least dreaming of making love in the latrines of Cologne, for there, as in the toilets of Tübingen I saw, if not an actual sexual encounter, auras of desire around the bodies of those who wanted to make love, and perhaps one aura would someday detach itself and mingle with the aura of some-one else who wanted to make love, and in that mingling of auras a third aura would arise that would bring the aura-less ones to-gether in the urinals of European metropolises. The urinals of European metropolises are cathedrals of love, as has been noted by anyone who has ever entered one, and while I stood in a WC in Stockholm I saw a couple worshipping in their own way, and while I leaned against the wall in St. Gallen I saw a young couple praying on their knees, and while I whistled in front of the latrine in Lenz I saw a man caress the sexual organ of the man next to him and noticed that no one stood next to me who might have caressed my sexual organ and felt then the previously mentioned emotion in this cathedral of Europe, this emotion that everyone must feel, I am convinced, as they enter or leave the pissoirs of Europe, these sanctuaries, fanes, basilicas of Paris, Rome, Leipzig, Oslo, Lisbon, Madrid. Children, too, must sense it, if only as a sort of future memory, but did I not also see several pairs of youngsters busy nuzzling and sucking one another in the chapels of Geneva? I did indeed. In train stations, museums, zoos, parks, airports, wherever I was in Europe I saw people wanting their sexual organs caressed, yanked, enfolded by mouth, ass, and vagina. And I saw, too, in several instances, these desires being acted on. In the cathedrals of Europe, i.e., in the urinals of Europe which in every way resemble cathedrals, I saw people praying before sexual organs, or if not actually praying, then playing with the sexual organs of men and women, no matter the age. I saw old men with old men, and young women with old women, and old men with young women etc., in the restrooms of Europe, and children, too, as I've said, there in these grottoes, caves, holes, their fingers seeking out other holes in which to enter, as one enters the caves of urinals, pissoirs, WCs of Europe, whether in Konstanz or Gdansk. These monasteries, for do they not also resemble in every way monasteries, are to be found in museums, parks, movie houses, and cathedrals themselves, cathedrals within cathedrals, narthexes where sex may occur in the dark, where, it is universally recognized, it should occur. Men meet men in the public urinals of Europe, and women women, and then they come together as is often their wont, to have flesh meet flesh, so that his flesh and her flesh or her flesh and her flesh or etc. might experience the flesh of the other against one's flesh, in the urinals, where such experiences often occur, so that desires can for once be acted on, in, e.g., the toilets of Montpelier. In the WC in the Schloss of Thun, overlooked by the castle's four turrets, I stood whistling at the latrine beside a young man who was also whistling, and for a moment our whistling matched each other's. His penis was out and my penis was out, and for a moment he looked at my penis, and I in turn looked at his penis and, for a moment, we contemplated each other's penis, contemplated what it would be like if he held in his hand my prick and I in my hand his prick, what it would be like if he placed in his mouth my prick and I in turn placed in my mouth his prick, what it would be like if he located within his ass my joint, and I in turn located in my ass his joint, what it would be like, in a word, for us to come together here in this WC in Thun, beneath the gaze of the castle's four turrets. But, for better or worse, the young man turned his eyes away, and at the same time I turned my eyes, and perhaps at that moment we both experienced regret for not acting upon our desires, as I have seen so many others do in the pissoirs of the European metropolises. In these cathedrals of defecation, so to speak, I have seen women, whose faces and hands were covered with liver spots, on their knees, and I have seen children of no more than eight or nine on their knees, and I have seen men my own age on their knees worshipping, so to speak, before the altar of their dreams. The opposite of loneliness is not easy to achieve, but I have seen it done in the dirty restrooms and the clean WCs and the filthy pissoirs in every city of Europe. These grottoes of excrement and love welcome us all. A stall door opens, someone enters. Humans are a shy species. I am leaning against the wall. In the public restrooms of Europe, more so than anywhere else, it may happen that our sexual organs are stroked, caressed, licked, devoured, and for once we know happiness.

$\mathcal{A}$ Fish Story

〜

Bob Zordani

My wife insists on watching me fillet the fish I catch. She brings her lawn chair out back while I hose the concrete slab I use to clean them on. She watches me intently, making sure to say how good I am with knives, how easy I separate the flesh from bone and slice the skin away. She likes for me to open up their stomachs and pull the contents out—half-digested crayfish, minnows, bugs, bait, and even plastic worms. If the stomach is empty, she tells me to turn it inside out so she can see the ridges which, to her, look like a brain. When I finish one, I hand her the fillets. She sprays them off, lightly, so they won't tear, and leaning down so I can see her cleavage, places them in the bucket. Then she fills it, swirls the water with her free hand, and talks to the fillets, telling them how nice they are, telling them to swim. She is serious, all the while looking straight at them and chanting her words. She gets sexier as she goes. By the time I finish, her cheeks flush and burn, but I just go about my business like nothing's happening. I watch her pull fillet after fillet from the bucket and shake each one until it's dry enough to carry in the house. I bury all the bones and guts and skin and take my time cleaning off the slab and putting up my gear, placing my rods along the cellar wall and straightening my tackle boxes. I smoke a couple cigarettes and close the cellar door behind me when I leave. The house is silent when I enter. The first un-cooked fillet rests on a plate smack in the middle of our foyer, and next to it, her shoes. I take the plate and follow her nylons up the stairs to the second plate. Two fillets, her blouse. I pile the fish on my plate. Down the hall, three fillets, her skirt. I pile the fish. The final plate's outside our bedroom door. Four fillets and her favorite lace panties. By now I'm sure she knows I'm standing there. She starts to coo and rustle on our bed while I kneel down and heap the last fillets on my full plate. I touch her panties, feel the moisture soothe my fingertips, and rub my nails back and forth against the door as gently as I can. She gets louder and wilder. I crack the door enough to watch her work. Her hands are skimming across her breasts, rippling her skin like wind over water. I feel faint and almost drop from excitement. Holding my plate, I swing the door wide open with my foot. I stare, I gawk, I ogle over her until she calls me in. I go to her and set the heaping plate between her legs. My clothes are sticking to my skin. I itch. She strips the top fillet from the pile, draws it down one leg, up the other, then up her stomach, around her breasts, her shoulders, and her neck, brings the meat to her mouth, kisses it, and licks it clean. It glistens in her hand. She puts it back and I lift the plate and put it on the floor. I fake a cast, pretend to bump an orange Salty Craw across the bed. She doesn't hit. I fake a cast and touch her with my hand. She quivers once and strikes so hard I think my arm will snap. I pull back hard and try to horse her home, but she won't come that easily. I have to work my way around the bed while she, with her hands around my wrist, rolls back and forth. When she's tuckered out, I pull that slick and gorgeous trophy in and look at her. She sighs a little, so I ask her what I ought to do with her. Now I've caught her, now she's mine. I grab her by the arms, holding them tight enough to settle her. I make her answer me. She says, *I'll do you favors if you let me go. Like what,* I say, and watch the color rising on her chest. She says she'll fan my spawning bed with her tail and keep the bluegill and the crayfish out. I tell her that's not good enough. She breathes in deeply and then it comes: She offers to fulfill my wildest dreams. I start to tell her that I love her, but she's all over me in nothing flat. Her mouth's on mine, and I can taste the fish she licked a little while ago. She pulls my T-shirt up above my head and yanks it off, and soon enough I'm naked to the bone. She says I've got the kind of worm she needs and takes me in her mouth. I fall back on the bed and tell her what a fish she is. She keeps on going, bobbing her head, twisting it until I'm ready to scream. And then she stops. *I want to spawn,* she says, climbing up beside me. I let her roll on top of me and tell me that she's lonely, that sexy fish like her are really sad and spend their days swimming by themselves in all the darkest coves which they can find. I kiss her neck and squeeze her to me. She kisses back. I tell her now, for real, that I'll swim with her through anything the years throw at us, through weather bad and good, through indifferent days and months when the whole sky is gray and overcast with doubt. I tell her that I love her, that I wouldn't let her swim alone through this lake's dark and tangled coves. We taste each other's grit and decide to go do it in the tub. We bring the plate and set it on the sink top just for luck, then turn the shower on and step in the tub. I grab a bar of soap and lather her down until she's slicker than a channel cat. She does the same for me, and we rub up against each other in the rising steam and let our lather mix like fish spunk as it swirls down our legs and drains away. Moaning like catfish, our bodies quaking, she lets me work my way into her. We go until we're spent and tangled together against the bathroom wall. The closest hand will shut the water off, and we will come apart eventually. But it's good to stand here, flesh to flesh, where we'll come clean in the easy water and make a plan for how to cook the fish. Maybe we'll bake or fry or broil it, serve it with a garden salad, potatoes, fresh beans, a bottle of chardonnay. I admit I like it spicy best of all because that's how I like to think of her: the way she tastes and feels, the way she moves when I come home and show her what I've caught.

Wonderland

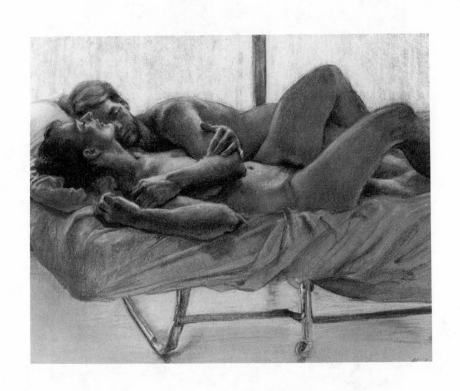

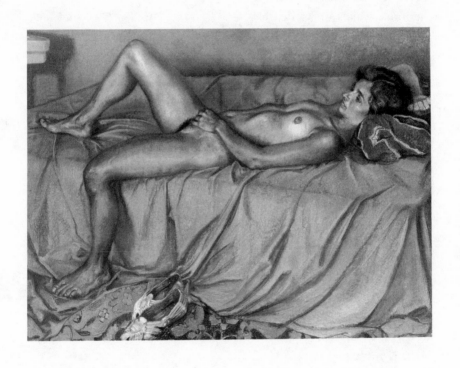

Owls

Louise
Erdrich

The barred owls scream in the black pines,
searching for mates. Each night
the noise wakes me, a death
rattle, everything in sex that wounds.
There is nothing in the sound but raw need
of one feathered body for another.
Yet, even when they find one another,
there is no peace.

In Ojibwa, the owl is Kokoko, and not
even the smallest child loves the gentle sound
of the word. Because the hairball
of bones and vole teeth can be hidden
under snow, to kill the man who walks over it.
Because the owl looks behind itself to see you coming,
the vane of the feather does not disturb
air, and the barb is ominously soft.

Have you ever seen, at dusk,
an owl take flight from the throat of a dead tree?
Mist, troubled spirit.
You will notice only after
its great silver body has turned to bark.
The flight was soundless.

That is how we make love,
when there are people in the halls around us,
clashing dishes, filling their mouths
with air, with debris, pulling

switches and filters as the whole machinery
of life goes on, eliminating and eliminating
until there are just the two bodies
fiercely attached, the feathers
floating down and cleaving to their shapes.

A Fisher of Men

Lee Durkee

Even in his earliest attempts Thomas Harper was a distracted fisherman, far more interested in scouting the azaleas along the bank for old wine bottles and condoms than in catching any of the pond's stock of bream or bass. All the fish had been hooked and released so many times that their mouths were laced with scars. The pond itself had been blueprinted by the architecture department on campus, stocked by biology, then landscaped with the mazes of azalea bushes by botany. Both of Thomas's parents taught at the college, a conservative school even by Mississippi standards. Like the rest of the faculty, the Harpers were provided with a house on campus. Their house happened to be next to the president's, a man who expelled students for what he termed public displays of affection, which amounted to holding hands. He would turn the names of expelled males over to the draft board. To a boy coming of age here, a boy whose parents sleep in separate bedrooms even, the wine bottles, the spread newspapers, the discarded Trojans, all of these held more lure than any fish that might follow a purple worm jiggled along the almost-perceptible bottom of a man-made pond.

Once a year the Harpers vacationed in Pensacola, emerging from the dark tunnel that ran under Mobile Bay onto a cat-walked bridge which would carry them still blinking into Florida. The upright fishing poles along the catwalk gave the bay a strobed effect as they drove; it made Thomas feel as if he were watching a film in which he could see the individual frames. He had a sister, Laurel, a year older, and both she and Thomas were allowed to bring one friend each on these summer trips. Thomas always chose his best friend Reese, a tall, sandy-haired kid graceful in ways that Thomas was not. Laurel never brought the same friend twice. The year of the drowning, a schoolmate canceled on her at the last moment and she did not bring anyone at all.

They arrived at the beach cottage late in the morning. By

noon the boys had shaken off their car naps and hit the beach, where the riptide flags snapped inland and storm clouds banded the horizon. Officially, nobody was allowed in the water, but as long as the sun held above the clouds, the tourists continued to make sandwiches and open beers and wade into the water waist-deep. The boys tried their hand at Frisbee, but on the fourth throw a gust of wind lifted the disk and carried it over a sand dune. They explored the dune, but could not find the Frisbee. So, after gaining permission, they rented poles at a nearby pier.

The pier had a bait shop at its base, all four walls peg-boarded with hundreds of fishing lures larger than any Thomas had seen before. To his disappointment, they were given some fish cut into strips and wrapped in white paper as bait with the rods they rented. When the man behind the counter winked at them, nodded at the bait, and said, "That there's for flying fish," he was met with twin deadpanned stares. The boys swaggered out, rolling their eyes. At the door Thomas even muttered, "Give me a break."

Cynical as they were, they did not stop until they reached the very end of the pier, where an old man, sun poisoned under a red baseball cap, was scraping the label off a gin bottle, seemingly in his sleep. His crab trap did not quite reach the water. The trap would sway in the wind and take prisoner the lines of neighboring tourists. The boys baited, cast, then pressed their groins against the rail and stared down at the line-crowded water. For a minute, Thomas imagined himself beneath the pier looking up at all the dazzling lures spinning and pinwheeling through the sky like kites. He kept imagining this even after Reese had begun to tell him, for about the tenth time, the story of a naked girl he had recently seen in a sorority window. More than to the story, Thomas listened to the words that Reese somehow got away with using, words that Thomas admired but that made him feel like an impostor each time he tried to use them himself.

"This chick was standing there, naked for all the world,"

Reese started, shaking his head. "And there was this cat in there with her. Behind her. Kinda dragging her away from the window, like peeling her off it, man. I mean, she was pressed against the glass, her body all kinda smeared the way little kids smear their faces, dig? I stayed there for hours looking up, daddy-o, thinking she's got to come back to me. Even after the lights went off I stayed there. My mom had the fuzz after me. By the time I gave up, my neck was stuck like this. I walked home staring straight up, man, up at the stars."

When it was Thomas's turn, he told a story about an azalea bush he had found one morning that was hung with dozens of used condoms. "Decorated like a damn Christmas tree," he said, shaking his head. Both boys were awed silent for a moment. "How exactly you figure that happened?" Reese finally asked, and Thomas just shrugged. "Dunno, man. But something's going on." He tested the weight of his rod, said flatly, "Though I bet I've looked in a million windows . . . never seen a damn thing."

"Yeah, but you got Laurel at least."

For the fiftieth time, Thomas sighed and tried to explain that Laurel didn't count. "She's my sister. If you had one, you'd understand."

"When was the last time you saw her, though? Half a year can make a difference. Look at me. I grew almost five inches last summer and gained sixteen pounds." Reese caught himself and too quickly added, "You just wait, chief. It'll happen to you, too, man. Quit worrying on it all'a time. I bet worrying slows it down some. I think I read that somewhere."

"Been reading a lot, have you?" Thomas said dryly. Reading was the one thing he did better than Reese. The truth was that Thomas was fed up with waiting. People had started to mistake him for Reese's younger brother. Distracted by this, he did not notice the short tugs on his line. When he finally hefted the rod, it bent straight down, and line went screaming off the spool. "Slower, slower," Reese coached him. "Tighten the drag—no—not—the other way, man—tighter, tighter." Thomas could not believe the weight of the fish. Here in Florida he felt anything might be hooked on the other end. Even so, after ten minutes of reeling, he was set back when something prehistoric looking broke the surface, gripping the line above the slipshod lure with one claw. Just about the time Thomas identified it as a crab, there was a streak of pink into the water, a splash, then the exaggerated weightlessness of the pole. Reese laughed while Thomas shook his head and reeled in the slack. "To hell with this," he said, setting down the rod. "Fish ain't the point. What we need is some of that." He pointed to the gin bottle in the lap of the sleeping man. "If we're ever gonna get any of that," and he nodded towards a group of girls in bikinis.

As if he had heard this, the old man with the bottle stirred and wiped the baseball cap over his eyes and then draped his arm across an opened styrofoam cooler beside him. The dozen or so blue crabs inside stretched their pincers towards him. He uncurled his palm to show the boys a chipped silver lure with yellow eyes. His palm was webbed with scars, and he was missing half a forefinger. The man drank a mouthful of gin and then dribbled a few drops onto the lure. He closed his fist and knocked three times on the pier. When he unfolded his hand again, the lure had been replaced by a silver minnow. The minnow flopped onto his lap and then fell through the spaced boards into the gulf.

"Shit," Reese said, and Thomas, fighting back a giggle, did his best to appear skeptical.

The man fingered the buttons on his fly thoughtfully. Then he set the bottle down and returned the cap to his head. He seemed disappointed in them. After a moment he began a series of violent coughs. When the coughs had subsided his eyes remained closed. The bottle was just sitting there.

The boys shrugged, rolled their eyes, shrugged again. Reese reeled in his own line, which came up snagged with a nest of old lures and braids of seaweed. He cut the line, then set the rod down and turned to survey the narrow pier, full of bait buckets and ice chests and rods and tackle boxes. "You run the obstacle course better," he lied. When Thomas heard this, he knew he would be the one to steal the bottle. "I'll turn these in," Reese added, gathering the rods. "We'll meet back up at the dune."

Laurel had spread herself onto a beach towel and begun work on her tan. She did not want Reese or anybody else for that matter to see her this pale. What she really wanted to do, what she would have dared Jennifer into doing with her, if Jennifer, that slut, hadn't backed out of the trip, was to undo their tops and lie with their breasts in the hot sand and watch the frat boys slashing Frisbees into the wall of sea gulls above the shell line. The Frisbees caught in the wind and sailed back inland, only occasionally landing in the water or brushing the thighs of nearby women. Two middle-aged women near Laurel poured themselves gin-and-tonics from a thermos and lowered their sunglasses periodically to catch the eyes of certain young men. Laurel sensed their disappointment each time a Frisbee missed their thighs.

"The only place he liked to do it, besides theme parks," one of the women was saying, "was telephone booths. He had this way of positioning us so that our feet weren't touching ground. Anytime I got him really hot, he'd start panicking around after a phone booth, like he didn't want to waste one on an elevator or a library or any *normal* place." A Frisbee landed nearby, and the woman stopped talking to lower her sunglasses. When she had caught the eye of its owner, she removed the lime wedge from her drink and squeezed the juice into her navel. The boy's mouth dropped, he scooped up the Frisbee, then darted into the water as if to drown himself. The woman shook her head sadly. "Where was I? Oh yes. Not that he was bad, mind you. I mean, in those phone booths we were actually above the ground, like birds, how many girls can say that? I never figured that man out until I was home visiting my parents. On New Year's Eve. My family had this stupid tradition, putting a dime in black-eyed peas. Whoever is served the dime is supposed to have good luck that year. Anyway, my Catholic aunts are all at the table, my father's had a few too many, as usual, and he starts telling this story. He's telling everyone about these obscene phone calls he's been getting at work. He's proud of them because they're coming from a woman. He's even got suspects from the secretarial pool. I don't think much of this—I mean, this is pretty much par for my father—until he starts doing an imitation of the woman who's been calling him. You know how I told you I start screaming out Hail Marys sometimes, and sometimes the Lord's Prayer? Well, that's what my father's imitating in the middle of New Year's dinner. My drunk father is imitating *my* orgasms. That asshole Eugene had been dialing my father's office all those times we were in phone booths. And right then, when all my religious relatives are being completely shocked by this, right then, I start to choke on the goddamn dime. And my stepmother, whom I detest, saves my life by using that goddamn new Hitler maneuver."

The women poured more drinks and willed the Frisbees onto them. Nothing about their attractiveness or the way their eyes followed certain boys seemed to differentiate them from any other woman around Laurel, who stood and let her vision follow the length of the beach. She got up her nerve then and sprinted out into the water. When it was up past her waist, she pulled off her bikini bottom and looked out at all the boys facing her. This isn't normal, she thought. Even for a virgin, I am not normal. There is nothing normal about me. She had begun to touch herself when a Frisbee splashed beside her and she almost screamed. She stared at the Frisbee a moment. Then, delicately, she transferred her bikini bottom to her left hand and blushingly flung the Frisbee overhanded back towards shore. It splashed into the water two feet in front of her.

That was when she saw her mother. Her mother was wearing a towel wrapped over her one-piece. Laurel had never in her life seen her mother swimming, not even in a pool. Laurel immediately started to pull the bikini bottom back on, but at that moment a monster wave hit her from behind and seized the suit from between her feet. After tumbling her around, the wave deposited her near the shore, and she had to backpedal like a crab to get herself below the water line again. From this position she watched her bikini bottom wash up on the shell line. One of the boys scooped it up inside a Frisbee and displayed it to his friend, who sniffed it then shielded his eyes and pointed out to sea. Laurel pinched her nose and slid underwater, forcing just enough air from her lungs to let herself lie flat on the sand, where she ballooned her cheeks as if trying to force her prayers up through the bright water into the gull-filled light.

As long as Dr. Harper could hear his wife yelling at their daughter, something about exposing herself to surfers, he felt safe rolling the marijuana cigarette in the cottage bedroom. The truth was he liked the daring of it. He had been given the marijuana a week earlier by an attractive graduate student whom he was considering having an affair with. Since then he had experimented with a couple of joints in his station wagon, and though he hadn't actually felt anything yet, he enjoyed letting the sweet odor pervade the car. In the kitchen, the resonance of his wife's voice increased then became conspicuously absent, only to be replaced a second later by the sound of his daughter crying. Dr. Harper spilled the marijuana onto the floor. He was sweeping it up with a *Life* magazine when his wife entered the bedroom.

"My God," she said. After a moment she added, "If it isn't Timothy Leary himself."

Tunneling the magazine, he poured the marijuana back into the plastic Baggie. "Are you interested in trying any?" he asked. "I promise not to take advantage of you."

If he did not necessarily feel on the defensive, it was because he had a trump card, an affair of his wife's that had come to his attention recently. Though he could not for the life of him imagine it was much of a physical affair—he knew both his wife and the head of his history department—he was certain that his wife would not make that distinction. It was all the infidelity she was capable of, so it was enough. He finished rolling the joint in front of her, then walked past her and shut the bedroom door. When he lit the joint, he blew smoke at her and laughed at how she leaped from its path.

"I am organizing a protest on campus," he told her. "To abolish the policy against public displays of affection. We are going to join hands around the pond. A chain of life. There will be placards and chanting and tie-dye and pot smoking and music and, hopefully, press. I'm going to try to enlist other faculty." He aimed another plume of smoke at her. "I don't suppose you or anybody else from drama would be interested?"

His wife answered as if she had had plenty of time to think it over. "You're up for tenure, Marshall. You throw that away, I'll leave you. You just watch me."

"I'm not interested in tenure, Mary. Don't you know that? I have this conflict with the department head. My only hope is that my wife puts in a good word for me." He winked at her. "Maybe on one of those late meetings." His wife started to speak, but he shut her up with another bomb of smoke. "Do you know why that buffoon keeps calling me into his office? To discuss the political nature of my history class. The political nature," he repeated, "of a history class." He snuffed the joint and tucked the roach into his shirt pocket. He had lost his train of thought. His mind was in a whirl, and he no longer wanted to argue. Finally he shrugged and announced that he was going for a walk, maybe catch up with the boys on the pier. He simply left it at that.

In the kitchen, his daughter was still crying. "It's okay, darling," he said to her. "When I first met your mother, she used to expose herself to surfers all the time. It's hereditary. Nothing you can do about it." Laurel only cried harder, which made Dr. Harper wince. "I was thinking of taking a walk to the pier. The radio mentioned the boys were catching swordfish the size of surfboards. Of course," he added, "you could always stay here with your mother."

Thomas knelt down and touched the gin bottle. Just as he started to lift it, the old man reached forward and stroked Thomas's thigh. Thomas tumbled over backwards, bottle in hand, then scrambled to his feet and took off down the pier, flying past the moon faces of fishermen, past the tackle shop, past Reese, who was handing in the rods. He heard Reese say, "Jeesus." The last two faces he saw before reaching the sand were those of his father and sister, but that did not register until he had the bottle tucked under his shirt and was sprinting along the shell line towards the dune.

Their dune was littered with bottles, magazines, dead fires, and disintegrating underwear; it had a tall bleach-white cross facing the highway. They had already stashed flashlights under their bunk bed in order to scout the dune that night and trace the source of these trash formations. When Thomas reached the dune he discovered that their special spot, an amphitheater-shaped bowl at the very peak of the dune, had been taken over by a group of college-aged kids who were tuning guitars and feeding driftwood into a fire. They were hippies, Thomas realized. Real ones, not like the half-asses in Mississippi. Under normal circumstances this would have been pretty intriguing, but Thomas was out of breath and in a hurry to stash the bottle. There was always the chance his father had not noticed it. A length of wire and picket fence surfaced and submerged throughout the dune like the spine of some sea creature. Thomas tunneled the bottle under this fence.

The beach had pretty much emptied. It was easy for him to pick out the small figures of his father and Reese walking towards the dune, Laurel lagging a few steps behind, adjusting her bikini straps again and again. Upon reaching the dune, Dr. Harper took off his shoes and started climbing. Reese and Laurel continued towards the cottage, but then Reese stopped to look up at where he knew Thomas would be. When their eyes met, their views became intertwined for a moment and Thomas was seeing, from where Reese stood, the reddish aura of the driftwood fire that capped the dune. He could see himself atop the dune, mostly the redness of his shirt. The spell broke when Reese turned to catch up with Laurel, and Thomas found himself back on the dune staring at the truncated sun, the distant slants of rain, his father walking towards him.

As he climbed the dune, Dr. Harper, still more than a little stoned, picked up trash. He did not look towards Thomas, but when they were next to each other, he knelt and transferred the trash onto the sand at his son's feet. "I don't care how curious you are about drinking, Thomas," he began, staring down at the rubbish. "What you did was to steal. I want you to understand what you're being punished for." He turned and sat so that his back was to his son. "Give me the bottle," he said. "Now." A moment later Thomas handed him a bottle with no label. He unscrewed the top and took a long drink. Gin. Very cheap gin. He shuddered, capped the bottle, looked out at the gulf, and tried to imagine what this place must have looked like to a DeSoto, what it was like to top one last dune and see the Gulf of Mexico spread before you. He thought about the poem by Keats that compared discovering the Pacific to reading a great book, and he thought what a silly comparison that was, how young it was. He took another drink. Finally he remembered his son and said, "Your mother has too much on her mind. We won't bring this up inside the cottage. See all this litter?" he asked, making a sweeping gesture with the bottle. "I'll drive into town for garbage bags. I want this place cleaned up. You're not allowed in the water until this dune is vindicated." Again he drank, but this time he held the liquor in his mouth until he reached a second conclusion. "And I want you to take this bottle back to that man on the pier," he said. He reached into his wallet and handed

Thomas a five-dollar bill along with the bottle. "Give him this, also."

Then Dr. Harper stood and stared back down, pointing to pockets of trash as he passed them. He was thinking about wisdom, about Solomon, about how punishment was the key to raising a good citizen, and as he walked he imagined all sorts of misdemeanors his children could commit and how best each of these should be punished.

Watching his father descend and considering his strange behavior and the alien landscape, it was easy for Thomas to imagine him as someone he did not know, an eccentric stranger on the beach. Thomas watched until the family station wagon had pulled out of the cottage driveway, then he quickly buried the bottle again and returned to the cottage, expecting a hero's welcome from Reese and his sister. They were sitting on the steps to the front door. Laurel was wearing cutoffs and a T-shirt over her bikini now. Her skin had already darkened, as had Reese's. Something about their intimacy there bothered Thomas. He held up his own white arms for inspection, then sat one step below them and decided to make them ask. They were divided as to the punishment. At first, it seemed too large a project, but the more they talked, the more they realized there was some liberation in it. At least they would be unsupervised, and they might be allowed to start work that night with flashlights. Laurel asked him where he had hid the bottle, and when he told her she nodded approvingly and estimated that if they worked hard they could be swimming by late tomorrow afternoon.

"It's not your punishment," Thomas told her. "Reese and I can handle it."

He had not meant to hurt her feelings. What he had in mind was their earlier project, that of scouting the dune. He just did not see his sister as fitting into that.

"She can come," Reese said. "We'll need all the help we can get."

The Book

"Not that it matters to me," Laurel added quickly. "Thomas can pick up all the garbage he wants. I've got better things to do. You know, I bet Daddy didn't even include Reese in the punishment. You didn't steal anything. Did he say anything to you about picking up garbage?"

"All he asked about was my grades, and did I support the war in Vietnam. Your old man's one strange cat."

"So you didn't actually do anything wrong?" she pressed him.

Reese shrugged and admitted that all he had done was to hand in the rods.

"Then why should *you* clean up *Thomas's* garbage?" she concluded.

What astonished Thomas was that Reese seemed to be considering this.

"Maybe he didn't have the balls to steal it," Thomas suggested. He stood. He had had about enough.

"Maybe I just wasn't that stupid."

Laurel laughed too loudly at this. When she had recovered, she said, "I think they might take the flags down soon. We could go swimming while Thomas picks up his garbage." Then she whispered, "They say everybody here skinny-dips at night."

"Y'all can both go screw yourselves for all I care," Thomas said, then flung open the screen door and let it slam shut behind him. His mother had been standing behind the screen spying on them. Her hair was let down, a rarity. It was black and straight with long strands of silver intertwined and Thomas thought she looked very pretty though a bit unrecognizable.

"Is your father acting strange? He didn't go swimming, did he?" she asked him. Thomas shook his head and said that he had driven into town. "He drove?" his mother said, securing the towel around her one-piece. "Well, I hope he doesn't kill anyone, that's all." She scrutinized the two teenagers on the steps, and then looked at Thomas again and shook her head. "Honestly, it's like y'all become different people the moment we set foot in Florida. I don't even know you."

Thomas went into the bedroom and took a nap on the bottom bunk. The trip down and all that had happened had caught up with him, and he slept without dreams and when he woke up he did not know where he was at first. Then he saw the carton of trash bags that had been left inside the door. When his mother called him to dinner, he pretended to be asleep. Reese came in to get something out of his suitcase, and Thomas kept on pretending even after Reese said, "You ain't asleep. You're faking, chief." Later he got up and pressed his ear to the door, but all he could hear was his parents, which meant that Laurel and Reese had actually gone swimming together. What was equally depressing was that his parents were arguing, not arguing politics as usual, but *arguing* arguing, so personal and violent that at first he thought it must have been on the television.

He opened the door and spied down the hallway that led into the kitchen. His mother was holding a pot of spaghetti sauce above his father's head. His father, sitting at the table, was daring her to go ahead and dump it on him. "Do it. God knows you want to," he yelled. There was no trace of humor in his voice, which was the strangest thing of all. "For once in your life do something. It'll make things that much easier for both of us."

Thomas stepped back into the bedroom and almost tripped over the trash bags. He grabbed the flashlight, then walked through the house and out the back door, letting the screen slam shut. He sprinted across the sand to the water and stopped there to regain his breath. Small red fires sectioned off the beach to either side of him. The white sweep of a lighthouse beacon moved over the water, then over the sand, then over him. Atop the dune, the spotlight at the base of the white cross flickered, went out, then returned. So many insects had been attracted to the spotlight that the cross seemed hallucinatory, like a splintered film of a cross being projected there. When the spotlight went out, the fires outlining the dune reddened, like cigarettes being inhaled. When it came on again, the spotlight reflected off the low clouds where the moon inserted itself periodically like a coin.

Thomas got to work. He worked feverishly, as if everything that seemed so wrong in his world could be remedied by simply filling trash bags. When he tied off a bag he left it along the fence. After almost an hour of this he had cut a channel to the top of the dune, and he sat down near the rim of the amphi-theater-shaped dell. He was covered with sweat, so he took off his shirt. It was the first time since he had been in Florida that he had been shirtless, and even in the dark he imagined that his pale bony chest was as visible as the white cross. Still, the breeze felt good. Below him, rising with the smoke of the bonfire, came the tuning of a guitar, and then the held note of a flute, clear and even disturbing. Lost in an absence of thought, he sat there until he heard a strange, guttural noise from below him. A couple had left the bonfire and positioned themselves unknowingly beneath where he sat on the rim. Even though he could barely distinguish whose limbs were whose, he watched the shadowy mechanics until the moon opened onto the sand and he could see the woman's hair and small breasts. His hand fell instinctively to his own groin. A moment later the woman's face rolled into the bar of moonlight and as Thomas came into his swimming trunks he recognized the face as his sister's. When this happened, he sat rigidly for a moment, sure that somehow he had been the one detected, and only when his own erection had subsided, which seemed to take forever, did he leap off the rim, landing on the opposite side of the lovers, and scurry down the dune.

He was working on his fourth trash bag since he had seen them when he came upon Laurel and Reese. They were singing "Let It Be," and Reese had an arm around her waist. Laurel was swinging the gin bottle. "Harp," Reese yelled. "Harp-man." When he made to slap Thomas on the back, Laurel crumpled onto the sand. Thomas shined the flashlight first on his sister, then directly in Reese's face.

"What'd you do to her?" he demanded.

"What'd *I* do to *her*?" Reese said, then laughed. "Turns out that ain't how it works, Harp."

Together, they dragged Laurel to the shell line so that the incoming tide rolled over her. Thomas had the theory that the water would sober her up.

"You got her drunk," Thomas stated. He picked up the bottle, drank it off, then threw it angrily out into the water. "You got her drunk with my gin," he repeated.

Reese grinned stupidly. "I ain't sure who got who drunk," he said, and put an arm around Thomas and started to describe what had happened. But Thomas removed the arm and told him to just shut the hell up.

"Who you telling to shut up, shrimp," Reese said.

Thomas hit him in the bridge of the nose with the flashlight and then fell on top of him, flailing at him with the sides of his fists. After a moment of this, Reese simply turned over and Thomas was trapped below his weight. "I ain't letting you up until you promise to behave," Reese said without malice. After a few minutes of this, Thomas agreed. They both stood and looked off towards the cottage's porch light. "If they catch us like this, man, they'll have us cleaning up the whole damn peninsula," Thomas said. Then something occurred to him. "I should just leave you two here like this," he said. But even as he said this, he noticed that the tide had moved in past Laurel's shoulders. He sighed and dragged her inland two feet.

"If I had a sister, man, I'd give her to you like that—" Reese snapped his fingers. "We could be brothers-in-law."

"Please just be quiet, okay? Please. I'm asking you nice," Thomas said. A moment later he said, "Look, I'm going to go check out the house, see if my folks are around. Maybe we can sneak her into her bed. You just stay here and keep an eye on things."

His father was standing in the shower of yellow light beneath the pull-chain bulb on the porch. At first Thomas thought his father was covered with blood, but then he remembered the spaghetti sauce. At that moment, the screen door opened, and his mother emerged carrying an armful of clothes. She walked past his father and stuffed the clothes into a half-opened window in the station wagon. His father did not say anything until she had wheeled around and disappeared back inside. Then it appeared as if he were arguing with the cottage.

"Encore, encore," he shouted, starting to applaud. "What's next, a few bars of Italian? Maybe a sword fight? Hey, call up the god-damned history department and tell Peterson to get his ass down here with a set of dueling pistols and a couple of powdered wigs. Would that be dramatic enough for you? You could sing a cappella while we pace off and shoot each other on the god-damned beach over you. Would you like that?"

The screen door opened again and hit him in the forehead. This time his mother carried an empty suitcase. It was unlatched and half of it trailed on the sand. She slung it into the front seat, then slung herself behind the steering wheel, then swung the car door shut. When she started the engine, Dr. Harper started shouting, *bravo, bravo.* He followed her the length of the oyster-shell driveway clapping and yelling *Bravo, Encore, Bravo, Encore.* When the station wagon accelerated, oyster shell flew through the air and he had to shield his face with his arms. *"Halt, cease, and desist,"* he shouted as the station wagon disappeared. *"Halt, cease, and desist."*

Thomas left him standing there and sprinted back to find Reese passed out on the beach, the tide almost reaching his feet. Laurel was gone. Where she had been was underwater now. Thomas attacked Reese's shoulders, screaming, "Where is she, man? Where the hell is she?"

Reese seemed to come awake instantly, throwing Thomas off of him and standing. For a moment he scanned the gulf in front of them. Then he screamed Laurel's name and charged blindly into the waves. Thomas followed, his flashlight slinging a bright wild lasso into the darkness as he swam. The last he saw of his friend Reese, ever, he was swimming with the riptide at an amazing speed. Thomas had broken away from the tide and was standing on a sandbar in chest-deep water, scything the flashlight beam back and forth over the gulf. He watched Reese disappear. Then very gently it began to rain. Behind Thomas, the rain fell on his sister, who had only crawled to the dune to be sick; it fell on his father, still in the driveway, hands clasped in front of him, who moved for the first time, cocking his head to squint into the storm. It fell onto the windshield of the station wagon, fell hissing into the driftwood fires, fell into a bucket of minnows left on the pier. He had lost a best friend. He had not lost a sister, though he did not know that yet. And what about his mother driving away? What had been lost there? He did not know what to make of it all. So he simply stood there, the rain falling in colors through the prism of his flashlight beam while a school of flying fish, attracted to that light, broke the water crazily all around him.

Twilight

Kathy Evans

He who loves what has been saved for the light
will awaken here near a woman who believes she will
someday die upon a salt beach next to a seal,
bearing no odors of a final decay. Something greek.

He will summon seabirds, and drop flowers on her flesh—
false heather, horn poppies, pale dune peas. Starfish
the color of dried blood will slide from the rocks
to cover her breasts; waves will roll over her wrists.

She will lift one hand toward the moon, as if to rub
an old scar, and out of respect for the darkness
he will obey the tide and fish from her white shores
until morning. They will make love slowly. It will be

the last time. The room, the beach, each small
estuary, her body, his mind, the swallows diving low
over shallow water, the white reasons for beds
and memorials, the music of mirrors, barking seals,

harpoon, the smaller compositions of dream, bone,
flowers cut loose on the sea, the habit, the order, the disorder, the whittled moon, all the anemones sucking her
name, the abandoned shells, his soft sea creature . . .

From this they will learn the limit of desire;
that the body is the only true place for exile; that there
is no horizon; that after swimming this far with driftwood in their mouths, they must enter the blue part of the fire.

Wonderland

Anthony Robbins

Come here, along the blue line,
past the state house, the aquarium,
under the harbor, by the airport, the memorial
beach: you with a solar music
box, dried fruits, odd mushrooms,
and a mouth harp. From the boreal
empirical, from the popular abstract, hardy and strange,
with a fellow adventurer, your co-creator, foundlings
in derbies and black leathers, come stumbling
through the oblivious mouth of a stranger's wedding,
through the doomed trees, come by the harbor
and watch the great glass catfish, their startling entrails,
roar down across the water. Or go inside the aquarium
to the corner where the eel flashes and hold
eternities there in each other as your hearts
hugely beat. *Come here* the voice
saying *follow your gloves, their ripped fingers*
along the beach explaining how you bore
the quotidian dangers of the left coast, how you were delivered
from the myriad guided suns. Come through
the bath of April and in the pied tub by the flickering
vase of fire azaleas with bubbles he will make
wing buds on your delicate shoulders. Be light.
Fly and be inlighted, tossing through the gale nights
with two hearts, with a small closed cry there in the dark
crook of thee. An old idea: that the journeying is
the land, that the line is only a line. But look
how the animal crawls out of the animal.
    At every moment. How the soul . . .

Walking In, Watching You

Jim Sorcic

I look away
amazed at how quietly
you come:
            one
finger pressed
against
the ragged chip
of your clitoris;
another
            sucked
up to the knuckle
deep inside

sweat breaks
                  salt-
water.

Makes
whole damn house
reek
      seaweed.

Eyes closed, two last
low moans, I look
for a window and face
the sky,
            the sea.

Say nothing.

Leaning
into your orgasm
like a bombardier
weeping
over the controls.

Michelangelo's Passion

Andra St. Ivanyi

As a young man, I spent each night cutting open the bodies of the people who had died in Florence that day. Unfortunately, they were mostly old men, their muscles cold and withered, jaws folding inwards.

Every night I made my way to Santo Spirito and waited eagerly for the sound of the Prior's robe to swish against the filthy back street stones. He pressed two fingers to his lips and led me to the shrouded bodies in the monastery morgue.

I looked forward to these evenings.

I am a sculptor, you see, and at the time I still needed to learn the nature of human sinew. How are our bodies held together? Which muscles are connected to which bone and with what? I needed to learn how the shifting of a limb causes one muscle to swell, another to contract, how the muscles on a man's stomach wave and untangle when he reaches above his head to receive the touch of God. Inhaling through my mouth, I stretched the skin back to reveal the layers of graying muscle beneath, and I stroked the cartilage with my fingers. I was young then, and I did this so that I could understand the nature of the human body.

And to try to understand the nature of human love.

To prepare for my sculptures, I sketched those bodies, young and old alike, until my sketchbooks grew fat and slipped into years. And I awoke longing for the feel of my file, my chisel, my coarse, wet rags, and I watched the blocks of inexpensive limestone take shape and slip into years as well.

But now the years have passed and gone. I am growing old. In Rome, no less. My brain is heavy with everything I know, my heart is heavy with everything I cannot feel, and I wonder if I am any closer to understanding the nature of human love.

My days are spent here on this scaffolding, a shaky affair of my own construction that I fastened to the ceiling with plaster wedges. At dusk my lamp matches the rhythm of my hand stroke for stroke, marking my slow progress across the ceiling in tiny heartbeats of light.

My face is stippled in the colors that have dripped from my brush. I am too tired to wipe them away.

Often my back aches in these cramped positions, and I steal minutes of sleep here. I dream of love, and of serpents wrapped around the trunks of trees, and of baffled old men, and of the varying degrees of shadow hidden in folds of cloth. Down below the Pope threatens me with his cane and raps his rings against my scaffolding.

"I will shake you down!"

I tense and prepare to fly as my scaffolding rocks and sways beneath me.

"I shall have you thrown down off there! Do you hear me?"

He wants me to hurry. Hurry! For this job, which I did not want to accept at all! I am a sculptor, not a painter. I see beauty in more dimensions than this flat fresco. And yet I agreed to the 3,000 ducats. So here I am, painting young and old alike, breathing the smell of wet plaster, going blind, and dreaming of the one I love.

If you have ever seen the ideal body, the weightless grace of rounded muscles! delicate lips! silken hair! then you understand the state of my rapture. You can understand me only if you have felt someone reach into your soul, and cup your heart in strong, safe hands that protect you as if you were a precious flame exposed to a windy night. Tell me, have you felt such passion?

Of course, I cannot express this love properly; the person who has inspired it does not know me, has not looked into my fevered heart. So instead I close my eyes to the burning inside and trust my charcoal, which hesitates and then draws images of Platonic love.

Platonic love is not less painful: when I open my eyes, I see

I have drawn vultures swooping down to devour the heart of a man who lies chained to a rock.

Tell me, have you ever felt such passion?

I'm floating, now, in deeper waters than these. On my knees before the altar, I press my knuckles into the soft whiteness of my beard, but I do not pray for the salvation of my soul. I pray instead for its relief, and the deliverance of my Love.

This is how I fell in love.

Above me Light had separated from Darkness, and I had moved on. Hovering over the immense waste of the seas was God, creating land out of the water. His hair and beard I painted gray and white, eyes closed, hands reaching outwards into emptiness.

I couldn't help it, that was what was in my heart.

In God's cloak huddled the souls of the unborn, naked, all of them. Outlining the slope of an unborn shoulder one morning, I heard a voice.

"Our Lord in Heaven, I beseech you . . ."

This was not so unusual. Many people came here to pray. They kneeled on the steps before the altar or sat on the bench against the wall, while above their heads panels revealing the Old Testament and the Era of Grace battled for their souls as the paint dried. They did not know I was there.

But this voice was different.

At first I did not pay attention to it as it floated past me as thin and innocent as a shadow. But then I paused, and I caught my breath, and I listened.

Below me someone confessed to a murder.

"I awoke this morning in the gutter of a foul-smelling street," the voice said, "with blood caked into my cuticles and 100 ducats in my pocket. I cannot remember how I came to be there, or who would beat me into such a deep sleep, or how I should come upon such an enormous sum of money."

I set my brush down in a bowl of water and turned onto my

stomach. Bowing before the high altar was a young man, who clutched his cap in tight, white fists and looked around him before continuing.

"I saw no blood, no corpse nearby, and I searched for a knife but found nothing." The voice broke and sobbed. "Have I truly robbed and killed a man with these two hands? I can't remember."

He wiped his face. Then he suddenly looked up in my direction, and I hardened where I lay so that he would not see me. I drank in the beauty of an angel. A thin nose. Strong legs. Eyes that glowed black with self-hate against the paleness of his skin. Oh! I can still remember the joy! I wanted to stretch my hands across the miles of air and stroke the golden waves of his hair. I wanted to press my hands against the planes of his perfect face. Already I could see the muscles of his chest underneath his tunic, and the heart that pumped defiantly there. As if in answer my heart pumped harder too, and begged me to preserve this beauty so it would last forever and never grow old.

His confession ended, the young man turned with such grace my bones turned to water as I watched. I tried to call out to him, I tried to touch his shoulder so he might turn around, but I couldn't. My tongue was a rock inside my mouth.

He left the chapel, and left me, and I sagged beneath the weight of my own need. But soon my skin began to loosen again. I rearranged my love for him to include his bloody hands.

How much can love forgive?

I do not know. I do not care.

Wait! Your name! I don't even know your name!

I tried to keep from drowning in the silence.

My obsession grew, expanding inside of me, as light as a cloud, yet so heavy I could barely move. I cannot explain it. I cannot string the right words together. Words, anyway, are empty things.

But the promises I made! I begged: Let me caress the white, hard block of marble, and take the same path God took across your flesh. I will connect bone to muscle to skin with my chisel and my sweat. I will scrape the edges smooth with diamond paper until you come alive, and when I am finished the world will gasp in admiration. But you will always be a child of mine, loved beyond all else.

So this is the nature of human love, bereft as it is of logic and virtue. Like sleep, it is another plane you ascend to, where you are warm and happy and out of control. Love grows inside you a promise at a time. Some say it is a gift from God. But then I ask Him, Why the sorrow? Why give the gift, and then take it all away? You love, you win. You love, you lose. You love.

Still, I fought my loneliness. I tried to work. Others came to pray—most often old women in silk dresses with wimples gathered loosely under their chins, who came wishing for rich men to marry their daughters. I did not hear them. They hissed out their prayers like snakes, but all I could hear was the absence of that one young voice. I kept hoping to hear it again. I prayed for his return. I ached for him.

How could I paint under those circumstances? Dull, heavy colors. Lines as stiff as my back. My hand could not copy the images in my mind. Plaster crumbled and fell into my eyes, and I cried.

I knew I must find him. At least, I must go look for him. I must fall on my knees before him and say, I have looked for you everywhere.

Then looking back at what I had just painted, I whitewashed over it in shame.

I am a sculptor, not a painter.

I climbed down off the scaffolding. I put away my jars of pigment and went to find him. I needed to paint and I could not paint until I had one more look. Just one. I would discover where he had come from, and what had really happened the night before. And then I would sculpt him from memory. My gift to the world.

But where does one look in this crowded city? Soldiers. Merchants. Artists with scarcely enough talent to fill an iron button on a cloak. Beggars, masons, pimpled apprentices who waste their small wages on cheap, sweet wines.

Where among them would I find him?

I am not a stranger to love. No. I was born hard and pure white, and it is not my nature to fall so quickly and so easily. The night I was to be born, my mother knew she would die, so she coiled her black hair onto her head and ran away to hide beneath the hills of Carrara. When the time came, she lifted me from her loins and kissed the bridge of my nose. How she loved me! Before racing back down the hill, she placed me into a vein of marble that swelled and flowed like a river of milk underground. From this I drank, and grew strong.

But soon my gentle mother died, leaving the earth as my wet nurse. I have worked my whole life to repay them both.

I understand what it means to be loved for no reason.

When I was nineteen, and ill with fever, a woman's cool hand stroked the hair at my temples and cooed me back to health. I can't remember what she looked like. I only know that her spinning voice suspended pain and gave me back my life, and I love her still.

The Search. Love can take us so far from everything familiar.

I passed the churches and the half-built palaces, the rubble and concrete ruins of antiquity. Into the foulest-smelling parts of the city, where filthy children as black as wolves tugged at my pockets. I walked along the banks of the river and looked for puddles of blood. I knocked on doors, I called up to balconies.

But perfection is hard to find and nearly impossible to describe; no one admitted to seeing a man of that description. No one knew of such a murder. No one could help me.

As I was heading back to the church, a boy dropped a squealing cat on me that tore at my face. I wet my sleeve with river water and dabbed at the scratches. I realized I was lost.

It was night, and nights in Rome are the blackest of anywhere on earth. If you lose your way, you will not find it again for years. Rumors tell of lovers who have stood next to each other at the appointed place and time, waiting for hours in the inky darkness without seeing each other. So I kept close to the Tiber. I sniffed it out in the darkness and listened to its gentle slurping.

And eventually I found my answer there.

Coming upon a fat boatman tying up his boat for the night, I offered him a gold florin to take me half a mile up the river. He stared at me with his pink, infected eyes and then helped me into his boat, taking care to lean against my body and make sure I was unarmed.

The river ran smooth that night. For an hour we did not speak. In the violet moonlight I could see the glimmer of the boatman's skin as he pushed us along.

Finally I cleared my throat. "Tell me, sir. Did you see a murder last night?"

He did not break his rhythm. He did not seem to hear me. So I asked again. And then I heard his voice answer me, even though I was watching his face and I will swear it did not move.

"I see murders every night."

I handed him two more florins and heard them jingle into a pocket hidden in the lining of his cloak.

Again he spoke, very very slowly. Again, his mouth did not move.

"Early this morning, three men tossed a body in the river. They did not see me, but I heard their laughter."

"I don't understand. Their laughter? Who were they?"

But the boat had stopped. We had reached our destination.

The Book

The boatman never lifted his waxy eyes from the water. I sighed and gave him my last florin. I would eat bread for the rest of the week.

The coin clinked and vanished. "They laughed about the poor young fool who would be hanged for the crime. They cracked open his head and left him in an alleyway, his pocket full of the Pope's gold."

A sour smell filled my head as I stepped up over the edge of the boat. Stumbling down the bank of the river, I heard him call out to me, and I turned around.

"I know something else," he said.

I shrugged. "I have no more coins."

"Are you the poor fool who will be hanged?"

I tried to steady myself, but my legs were weak. "Tell me what you know, old man, or let me go."

The boatman gripped his oar tightly and began to push away from the bank. Silver rings spread outwards from the boat. His voice was a whisper that scraped against my skin.

"The man. They killed. It was the Archbishop."

And that was the truth. In a few days the missing Archbishop's body swelled with blue gasses and floated to the surface of the river, throwing all of Rome into an uproar. It seemed in those days that no one of any prominence could die a natural death. Some men ran with torches through the city shouting curses through their fists. Others celebrated, tossing olives in the air and catching them between their teeth. I sat upon my scaffolding and mixed my pigments and listened to the Signory below hiding their chuckles in their sleeves.

But the wicked clergy below did not bother me. I had my answer. And I would see the man I loved again. Let the cardinals and the bishops commit their murders—I would not help them. I would not allow an innocent man to hang. So I invented a plan to save him.

When we're in love, we feel so powerful, so strong. Oh, the

battles we are prepared to endure! But the truth is, we are naked in our love. As weak as mewling kittens. We do not realize the enormous odds we are up against, (but even if we did, we would risk it anyway). We think our actions make a difference, as if one bold move or clever plan could rescue us from loss and loneliness.

You love, you win. You love, you lose. You love.

I'll tell you my plan:

I painted. The next three days I painted wet plaster and watched a God who did not answer my prayers appear beneath the fibers of my brush.

But my nights? Ah, those belonged to me and I chose to give them to my obsession.

Sleep caused my stomach to pinch. I did not eat or drink or say a word to anyone. Instead I worked deep inside the bowels of the church. Creamy marble with sparkling silver veins. I heard a voice inside it begging for my touch, I saw inside it a head thrown back, an expression of joy, the face of Love. Sweat dripped from my eyebrows and was held in shining arcs beneath my eyes. My skin cheeks grew waxy and red with fever. Still, the marble was cool when I pressed my forehead against it. It whispered to me, and I obeyed. I stroked and patted it with my mallet and chisel until it trembled to life.

A few days later, of course, they found him. A man beaten free of his memory, a man at the mercy of the Church itself, of course they found him. And he did not lift an arm to protect himself as the family of the dead Archbishop, dressed in white hoods, dragged him through the streets and beat his back with lances.

"Who paid you to kill? How can you not know?" they shouted.

When they reached the hanging square, I was already there,

waiting. I had heard their shouts, and I was ready. When the Pope on his horse came to see the shameless thief for himself, I stopped him. I waved my hands above my head like a madman and fell to my knees in front of him.

"Stop!" I shouted. "Oh Most Holy Father, you must stop! This man is innocent!"

The cardinals, the priors, the bishops in their red cloaks stopped to stare at me. The painter! they cried. What does he know? they cried. These proud men had paid good money for the Archbishop's life. They glared at one another with angry questions in their eyes.

"This man," I cried, pointing to him. "He could not have killed our beloved Archbishop," I pleaded. "Because he was with me!"

The crowd started to snicker, nudging at each other and pointing to me. A fool! Look, a fool!

But I knocked down the boards that had stood around my masterpiece, and it was born, as I was, hard and pure white. The angry crowd quieted. The Sleeping Captive arched upwards to the heavens, one arm raised, the other resting gently on his chest. The muscles on his stomach waved and untangled perfectly as he reached above his head to receive the touch of God.

The crowd listened to the marble breathe. They willed the statue's eyes to open, the lips to part. Then they looked at the prisoner and started to whisper again.

Their faces were identical.

"He was with me!" I said, catching my breath. "With me! He modeled for this, for your memorial tomb, Father. The very one Your Holiness commissioned. He was with me!"

The Pope's eyes stabbed at me as he helped me to my feet. "But what of the chapel?" His voice rose. "You should be working on the ceiling of my chapel!"

"But I worked only at night. This marble is my first passion, my strength. Without it I cannot paint."

But then a voice cried out (an angry prior, maybe one of the assassins himself!), "But it could be an old statue. You could have carved it years ago!"

The Pope himself came closer to look. He walked around the figure several times and shook his head.

"It is new," he said. "I have not seen this piece before."

And I saw disbelief brighten the faces of the Signory. And then anger darkened them again. They opened and clenched their fists. But what could they do?

These men, you see, understood little about love and knew nothing of my memory.

The Pope ordered the statue to be placed with the others commissioned for his tomb. He shook a finger at the bridge of my nose.

"No more sculpting until my chapel is complete!"

I swallowed my pain. I bowed my head and promised.

But my humility was rewarded. The Pope pointed at the prisoner and barked, "Let this man go and continue your search."

My masterpiece was taken away.

And my love was released. He looked at me in astonishment. He watched his stone likeness being wheeled through the streets towards the Pope's tomb. Confusion tripped across his face and caught in his throat. I wanted to explain.

Please! I cried to him across the square. Understand, I did not save you for the truth. I did not save you for you. I saved you for me.

But he did not hear me. He could not see me pleading with him. A woman with braids around her ears wiped his face with the hem of her skirt.

Please! I cried.

The townspeople dripped away in disappointment, pulling their yelping children behind them. A curtain of sky dropped so low it brushed the top of my head.

And when I blinked he was gone, and I was all alone again.

⌒

So this is the nature of human love. I have learned that my body is held together with hope. The hope that I will see him again, that I will be gripped by such beauty again. My muscles are connected to my bones with the promise of love.

I paint and paint, my eyes inflamed and red. So here is where you found me, crouching high atop my scaffolding, shivering in the dark, warmed only by the heat of my obsession.

I paint.

Above me Light struggles to separate from Darkness. There, hovering over the oceans, is God. His hair and beard have grown gray and white in understanding and acceptance. Still, his eyes are closed in pain. His hands grope outwards in hope.

This is what is in my heart.

Milkflowers

Robert Wrigley

It is first that angle at which you sleep,
canted, neither on your back nor your side
but in between. The baby, fallen asleep at last,
must let go his latch, and your nipple
gummed these months to impossible softness
slowly oozes one sweet delinquent drop.

But sweet as it is, I don't take it,
because it is not that richness I crave
but its ghost, glimmering silver in the light of candles,
dried by my breath softly blowing . . .

Thus, when the baby is tucked in his cradle,
I lick my lips and kiss your milk-anointed breasts
until my mouth is glazed with the purest sugar,
then knead from each nipple one additional drop to dry,
and begin, all down the trellis of bones,
to paint your skin with invisible roses.

The Moment the
Two Worlds Meet

Sharon Olds

That's the moment I always think of—when the
slick, whole body comes out of me,
when they pull it out, not pull it but steady it
as it pushes forth, not catch it but keep their
hands under it as it pulses out,
they are the first to touch it,
and it shines, it glistens with the thick liquid on it.
That's the moment, while it's sliding, the limbs
compressed close to the body, the arms
bent like a crab's rosy legs, the
thighs closely packed plums in heavy syrup, the
legs folded like the white wings of a chicken—
that is the center of life, that moment when the
juiced bluish sphere of the baby is
sliding between the two worlds,
wet, like sex, it *is* sex,
it is my life opening back and back
as you'd strip the reed from the bud, not strip it but
watch it thrust so it peels itself and the
flower is there, severely folded, and
then it begins to open and dry
but by then the moment is over,
they wipe off the grease and wrap the child in a blanket and
hand it to you entirely in this world.

Love in Blood Time

Sharon Olds

When I saw my blood on your leg, the drops so
dark and clear, that real arterial red,
I could not even think about death, you
stood there smiling at me,
you squatted in the tub on your long haunches
and washed it away.
The large hard bud of your sex in my mouth,
the dark petals of my sex in your mouth,
I could feel death going farther and farther away,
forgetting me, losing my address, his
palm forgetting the curve of my cheek in his hand.
Then when we lay in the small glow of the
lamp and I saw your lower lip
glazed with light like liquid fire
I looked at you and I tell you I knew you were God
and I was God and we lay in our bed
on the dark cloud, and somewhere down there
was the earth, and somehow all we did, the
blood, the pink stippling of the head, the
pearl fluid out of the slit, the
goodness of all we did would somehow get
down there, it would find its flowering in the world.

Divinity

Divinity

Galway
Kinnell

When the man touches through
to the exact center of the woman,
he lies motionless, in equilibrium,
in absolute desire, at the threshold
of the world to which the Creator Spirit
knows the pass-whisper, and whispers it,
and his loving friend becomes his divinity.

Last Gods

Galway
Kinnell

She sits naked on a rock
a few yards out in the water.
He stands on the shore,
also naked, picking blueberries.
She calls. He turns. She opens
her legs showing him her great beauty,
and smiles, a bow of lips
seeming to tie together
the ends of the earth.
Splashing her image
to pieces, he wades out
and stands before her, sunk
to the anklebones in leaf-mush
and bottom-slime—the intimacy
of the visible world. He puts
a berry in its shirt
of mist into her mouth.
She swallows it. He puts in another.
She swallows it. Over the lake
two swallows whim, juke, jink,
and when one snatches
an insect they both whirl up

and exult. He is swollen
not with ichor but with blood.
She takes him and sucks him
more swollen. He kneels, opens
the dark, vertical smile
linking heaven with the underearth
and licks her smoothest flesh
     more smooth.
On top of the rock they join.
Somewhere a frog moans,
     a crow screams.
The hair of their bodies
startles up. They cry
in the tongue of the last gods,
who refused to go,
chose death, and shuddered
in joy and shattered in pieces,
bequeathing their cries
into the human mouth. Now in the lake
two faces float, looking up
at a great maternal pine whose branches
open out in all directions
explaining everything.

Speaking in Tongues

Carson
Reed

I remember the preacher said: "Let them be joined together forever in the Holy Spirit," and I kind of wrinkled my brow because God is easy and Jesus is easy but the Holy Spirit thing was always way beyond me, and I wasn't really sure that what I had in mind was a ménage à trois with some supposedly benevolent essence, and in my poor agnostic head I imagined the two of us suspended in the spiritual plasma of the Holy Ghost for eternity, like watermelon pickles.

But when we headed out of the old adobe church that day so far as I could tell it was still the two of us, just you and me, light-headed as teenagers in the summer in the evening in the park, our vows an exotic narcotic wrapped in plastic and shoved down deep in our socks.

And I remember we didn't even make love that night, but consummated our marriage in the deep sweet of sleep. In the morning there were tiny roses of blood on the bed and I knew that my dreams had ferried across the occult water of sleep and with a broad flat sword had broken through the soft dense flesh of your maidenhead to dance with you to the beat of feral drums.

And when the morning had come, sure enough, there was the Holy Spirit, less like a poltergeist and more like a cat, perched on a comforter on the old steamer trunk at the end of the bed.

"Go ahead," the Holy Spirit dared me. "Touch her." And I touched you and the walls shuddered like an old miner's shack teetering into the San Andreas fault.

"Holy shit," I said, thinking this could be dangerous, and then I realized that I had blasphemed and I was afraid and embarrassed.

"It's okay," the Holy Spirit told me. "You go right ahead. Don't worry. Nothing can harm you."

So I kissed your ear, and Aretha Franklin began to sing.

And I pulled off your T-shirt and the bed danced a samba across the floor.

And you said "That's cool," and I said "You try it" and you kissed me on the lips and instantaneously the bedroom walls shattered, covering us in gypsum dust and little puffs of pink insulation and bright shards of glass.

I cupped your breast in my hand and bit at your nipple and the trees moaned with pleasure and all the neighborhood children gathered around us in the rubble and danced in a ring, their little hands holding each other gingerly like hamsters.

I touched your belly and Gideon appeared, his trumpet blasting a Hallelujah into the quivering sky.

Then you pulled hard at my back and fire roared down from the sky like napalm, sucking the air from my lungs and smoldering in jellied splotches on the soles of my feet.

I stroked your side and buck naked laughing seraphim appeared fluttering all around me, randomly shooting morphine-dipped arrows into my butt.

Light stuck to your naked body like a fresh-cut haystack after a rain. You looked just like a desert sunrise and you tasted just like filé gumbo and you smelled just like the spray from the breakers at Patrick's Point.

Puppies played under your skin and some unseen hand snaked a length of hairy twine up from my tailbone and out through the center of my skull, harmlessly pulling out bits of unused brain tissue that stuck to my hair like marshmallows.

And when I pulled your thighs apart the sky opened and God himself came thundering down wearing a porkpie hat with a press pass stuck in it, taking a seat at the announcer's desk of some celestial sky box, surrounded on every side by bleachers full of rowdy drunken angels.

"Don't mind Me," He said into the microphone.

And then He filled us so full of the Holy Spirit that It oozed out of us and we slipped and slid across each other, the Holy

Spirit sticky in our mouths, the Holy Spirit leaking liquid blue light from our fingertips, the Holy Spirit trickling down our foreheads and stinging into our eyes, the Holy Spirit pouring from our armpits and off our legs and our shoulders and from between your legs and making a Holy mess on the bed.

We were speaking in tongues. We were rolling holy rolling in the sheets, our tongues were driven mad with Pentecostal ecstasy, our tongues were epileptic, our tongues were frothing, our tongues were crying, our tongues were screaming, our tongues were babbling holy nonsense, our tongues were repentant of every sin, our tongues praised God, our tongues were baptized, our tongues were washed with the Blood of the Lamb, and our tongues were born again. And again.

And as our tongues gave witness to the power of the Holy Spirit, I heard the strange words rise up into Heaven and rattle the very cage of the universe, building, like an argument, shattered, like the Tower of Babel, resurrected, like Jesus, emerging from the dark cave of our souls.

And then it was night again, and the Holy Spirit settled down on us like a feather comforter, a soft weight that pulled us close in the night, down toward the dark beat of drums around a fire in the forest along a turgid river of sleep.

And as I drifted slowly down from the headwaters of the Holy Spirit, I remembered what the preacher said: "Let them be joined together forever in the Holy Spirit," and I pulled you closer and murmured from my tired, tired tongue, "Oh, baby, amen."

Redundancies

Stephen Corey

So we move to moisten
what is already damp,
to wet what is already moist.

Shadows in hand
we trace the traced.

What is hot we heat—
what is open, open wide—
what filled fill again,
spill over, and fill.

The risen we raise,
the plumbed we sound.

Already posed,
the positions hold—
what was there
is there once more.

Jesus of My Youth

Sarah Brown
Weitzman

Every Sunday
he hung life-sized
at the end of my pew
long and white
but for the blood at his head
his right side,
and where he was nailed to the wood.
A blush of lipstick
no nun could scrub away
had seeped into the porous plaster
where women worshippers kissed his feet.
Each time I put my mouth
above the spike
to his cool hard foot,
I thought of real flesh
and when the others bent
for the benediction or to be blessed,
I followed instead
the arc of his ribs,
the line of his limbs
the sculptor had shaped so well
that even then, O Lord,
even then I was lost
in the beauty of men.

The
Sculptor
of Eve

~

Sarah Brown
Weitzman

"God formed
man of the dust
of the earth."

Genesis 2:7

But when God wanted a woman
he did not start with dirt
but the smooth, clean curve
of rib, perfect
except for the broken end,
working it up
into her against the smell of musk
melons in the humid air
of the garden.

Eve took him
into her night. The moon floated
out of his left eye. Those
vast unpracticed fingers
slipped. All women bleed
with the moon tides
of that first biology.
Did something rise in him then?
The idea of making her
for himself?

As he laid her
across the colossus of his knees
to carve the long line
of spine down to the bottom
of her back, he was concerned now
with symmetry, the balance
of buttocks with breasts,
how to give her two mouths.

Slow work then
to dig out a passage for pleasure,
a crevice as wonderful
as thunder, as dangerous
as a fault in the earth,
as tinged as the ripened skin
of the innocent apple.

The
Groundfall
Pear

Jane Hirshfield

It is the one he chooses,
yellow, plump, a little bruised
on one side from falling.
That place he takes first.

Rapunzel, Rapunzel, Let Down Your Hair

Jancis M. Andrews

These autumn days, morning opened softly along the Washington coast, always with a lingering mist, so that even at ten o'clock, the sun hung in the air like an altar lamp seen through smoke. And the trees, Ruby noticed, waddling towards the herb garden, were filled with migrating birds. At first, in ones and twos, then in small groups, then in one long continuous movement, so that they were like a long, living skein drawn out of the earth, the birds would mount the sky and turn: a communal heart beating unhurried and purposeful towards the south. She would watch until the whole high dream of them had blurred into the sun, and when she looked again to earth, part of her felt missing, flown with them to another country. At such moments, all things became sharper, etched: the fennel: a green spear piercing the pale gauze of the sky; the parsley: sprays of darkest green foam; the chive flowers: little lavender heads softly tonguing her fingers. Her hands began to tremble. I'm really upset today, she thought; that couple in the park really upset me.

The scent of basil clung to her hands like an offering of spiced earth. Deciding she had sufficient for the salad, she rolled to where the green-nippled rosy globes of the tomatoes nestled among furred leaves of shadowed green. From here she could see into the sitting room, where her employer, Mrs. Lee, was talking to the luncheon guests. One of them—the son of one of Mrs. Lee's friends—was staying overnight before returning to Seattle. His name was Robert, a name that suited him, she thought, remembering other Roberts from her reading: Robert the Bruce, Robert McGregor: the Rob Roy, Robert de Guiscard, Duke of Normandy. In her mind's eye, men named Robert were tall, with the look of the warrior-poet about them; they had expressive eyes and lips that hinted at a passion in them that corresponded to the passion within herself, and their bodies were lean and powerful

—like the visitor's, she thought, glancing covertly at his slim hips as she passed by the French windows.

Ruby herself was grossly obese. That was her mother's phrase, proffered in worried whispers to pediatrician after pediatrician: "grossly obese." Ruby did not keep a full-length mirror in her room; it was sufficient that her doctor kept one in his surgery. It was on these weekly visits that she was brought face-to-face with the flesh hanging in swathes from underarm to wrist, with the breasts like a cartoonist's joke, with the belly and buttocks like great barrels hasped in fat. She looked defiantly at the tomatoes nestling in her hands. I'll make a soufflé to go with the salad, she decided, and to go with it I'll make the lightest, crispiest rolls I've ever made in my life. Waddling into the kitchen, she placed the basil in a jug whose pale green china complemented the herb's vivid green; arranged the tomatoes in a blue dish in order to enjoy the contrast in colors; then got out the bread bowl, flour, and yeast.

"You're rightly named Ruby—you're an absolute jewel. You'd make someone a wonderful wife." That had come from old Uncle Edward as, suddenly misty-eyed, he had patted her on the shoulder when she had visited him last Sunday, bearing one of her special sponge cakes. She had stammered something in reply. Never before had a member of her family paired her with the opposite sex, and now here was Uncle Edward actually suggesting . . . God, this flour feels just like silk, she thought, her fingers caressing the contents of the bread bowl. When Mrs. Lee suddenly opened the door, Ruby jumped, as if she had been snatched back from a far place.

"Ruby, Ruby!" Mrs. Lee laughed. "My dear, your nerves! Are you all right?"

Just a slight accent, Ruby thought: delicate, like the print of birds' feet in Chinese paintings, like Mrs. Lee herself.

"Yes, yes, I'm fine. You just startled me a bit, that's all."

"I wanted to ask—are you sure you would not like this

evening off? After all, it is your birthday. I can always ask Mary."

"It's all right. I wasn't planning to go anywhere, anyway."

It didn't come out in quite the casual way she wanted, and she saw Mrs. Lee pause before commenting, "Forgive me if I'm intruding, my dear, but these last few days, you have seemed rather tense, not yourself. Is anything wrong?"

Mrs. Lee's feet, Ruby saw, were fine-boned and fashionable in shoes that were airy webs of white straps over a slim high heel, shoes such as she herself would never wear. Her shoes had to be specially ordered, and were made of thick slabs of leather in order to support the slabs of flesh they enclosed. And Mrs. Lee was wearing a flowered dress cinched in at her tiny waist, while Ruby was wearing one of her usual homemade sacks: a navy-blue monotone, because, according to women's magazines, bright colors and pattern added bulk.

She said coldly, "I thought I'd make a terrine for dinner to-night. It's a French dish, quite difficult, so I'll need time to pre-pare it."

"You are the mistress of the kitchen, Ruby. Are you quite sure there is nothing wrong?"

"Well . . ." Ruby hesitated. It was no more Mrs. Lee's fault that she had been born a pink-and-white porcelain miniature of a woman, than it was Ruby's fault that somewhere in her fam-ily's history a defective gene had slumbered, then awoken to gar-gantuan life in her. And Ruby had to admit that Mrs. Lee was always gracious . . . She stammered, "As—as a matter of fact—something did happen a couple of days ago."

"Something unpleasant?" Mrs. Lee was concerned. "My dear Ruby, you must tell me."

"It was so unexpected." She hesitated again.

"Yes?"

"I was taking a shortcut through the park, and I came on this young couple . . ." She paused, and bent low over the bread bowl so that when she spoke again her voice echoed hollowly from the white china interior. "They were both naked . . ."

"Good Heaven!" Mrs. Lee's almond eyes widened. "And they were—"

"Yes, they were." Heat mounted the folds of fat on Ruby's cheeks. "I was really shocked."

"I should think so! In a public park! But I would certainly not let such a thing trouble you, Ruby. That is their low moral standard, not yours, after all."

"It was just that it was—so unexpected," Ruby mumbled.

The boy and girl had been making love in a grassy hollow near a stream. The sun had lit brilliantly the whiteness of the boy's naked buttocks and back, the strong arch of his shoulders, the muscles swelling in his upper arms, his fair head moving from side to side as his lips sought those of the girl while moving into her; the girl herself, her body a glimpse of gold, her blond hair tumbling over the boy's arms, had been lifting her hips rhythmically and urgently to his, thrusting up with her feet strad-dled wide in the tall grasses, her arms locked about the boy's neck, her lips and tongue moving passionately under his. Their coupling had been fierce. She had not guessed it would look like that. There had been a wildness in the wind pressing against the surrounding trees, a wild music of water cascading over rock, a wild sweet scent of crushed grass. She had walked away as noise-lessly as she could. . . .

Blindly, she reached for the mixing spoon, but it clattered from her fingers to the floor. Mrs. Lee picked it up.

"I think we should have a wine-based dessert for dinner to-night," Ruby said loudly, retrieving the spoon. "Something sharp but sweet to the palate."

"Whatever you think best. I just came in to tell you that I shall be showing the garden to my guests. How handsome Rob-ert has grown up to be—I remember he was always such a kind boy—a little impetuous, maybe, but so kind. Mr. Lee will be sorry to have missed him."

Mrs. Lee smiled and clicked her high heels to the door; then paused with her hand on the handle. "Do not bother yourself about the couple in the park," she said. "They are simply not important." The door closed behind her.

Ruby lowered herself onto the big, custom-built stool her parents had given her on her last birthday, and began stirring the warm yeast mixture into the flour. As she breathed in the creamy redolence of the yeast, a hairgrip loosened, and she felt her hair beginning to slip. Heaving herself up, she rolled over to the mirror fixed above the kitchen sink. Sure enough, one lone curl had escaped from the masses of hair piled on top of her head: a curl of tenderly shadowed gold, rich and silken. This was the incredible comparison: a grossly obese body, topped by a glistening profusion of golden hair as lavish and as sumptuous as a pagan feast. She maneuvered the hairgrip into position, and lumbered back to the stool.

Luncheon was over; all the guests except Robert had departed, when the kitchen door opened and Mrs. Lee entered, Robert close behind her. Ruby was bent low over *Bon Appetit*—one of the disadvantages of having fat clotting the eyelids—it interfered with the vision, just as her stomach interfered whenever she wanted to stand near the table or the sink. Her sacklike cheeks, and the tires of fat that comprised her throat, were flushed from the heat of the oven. Perspiration had broken out in spite of the liberal sprays of antiperspirant, and her navy sack dress had enormous half-moons under the arms. It was always like this, as if her flesh worked hugely and continually at melting itself down.

"You didn't meet Robert properly at lunchtime," Mrs. Lee said, "and I know he wants to thank you for that delicious soufflé. This is Robert Mansini, and Robert, this is Ruby Anderson, the best cook in Vancouver."

"Happy twentieth birthday," said Robert, and took Ruby's hand.

"Why, thank you," she said. From habit, she steeled herself for the usual repelled reaction, but the blue eyes looking into hers were serene and smiling. It was, she thought, shocked, almost as if he had not noticed her size—or that if he had, it did not matter to him. She was not aware that she was repeating "Thank you, thank you," while she stared at him. What a wonderful-looking man, she was thinking, so tall, so alive-looking. Look at those blue eyes and that black hair. My God, he's absolutely gorgeous.

"My parents came from northern Italy," Robert smiled, "and I'd always thought the best cook in the world was my mother. Now I've met someone whose cooking rivals even hers. Thanks for giving up your evening for me, I really appreciate it." And he bent his dark head over her hand and kissed it.

Ruby could not speak. Her face shone in its fat.

"Ruby is making you a special dish tonight," Mrs. Lee said. "And now, Robert, I take you into town. You can manage all right, Ruby?"

"Yes, " Ruby whispered.

"See you later, then. And thanks again for giving up your birthday for me . . ." Robert hesitated. Ruby did not know of the brief, low conversation that had taken place in the dining room, when one of the guests, inevitably, had mentioned Ruby's size. Mrs. Lee had murmured she found it strange that Ruby had chosen cooking as her career—obtaining a diploma from the Cordon Bleu School of Cookery, no less—when she herself was limited to a sparse diet, and pills. "But Ruby is a fighter," she had added, "maybe that has something to do with it. And she is quite the artist—she can make a dish look like a still life." She had also mentioned—although she immediately wished she had not—that people like Ruby often died young. The thought of anyone dying young had upset Robert. Now, because he was deeply sorry for her, because, in spite of himself, the sight of Ruby's fat had impelled the word "gross" into his mind, the smile he gave her was brilliant, almost tender. He searched around for something nice to say. "You know," he said, "your hair is really very beautiful. You should show it off."

"Oh, it is, it is beautiful," Mrs. Lee cried eagerly, for the sense that she had revealed too much about Ruby was still with her. "I have seen it once or twice, when she is washing it. It is like the hair of a princess, like a carpet of gold." She laughed, pleased with the image that had just slipped into her mind. "You can fly away on her hair," she said.

Robert reached out and very lightly, as one might a child, touched a rich swathe that curved above the ribs of fat on Ruby's forehead. "Rapunzel, Rapunzel," he quoted, "let down your hair."

All the curtains and folds of flesh that were Ruby's cheeks and chin flushed a bright, disordered pink. She looked confusedly at him. He took her confusion to be ignorance of the fairy tale.

"The princess in the tower," he said, smiling. "Remember? She let down her beautiful hair so that the prince could climb up and rescue her. Your hair reminds me of that princess." And lightly, lightly, he touched her hair again.

"Yes, your hair is your beauty," Mrs. Lee smiled. She had nearly said, your one beauty, but had stopped herself just in time.

"Do we go in my car or yours, Robert?" she asked.

"Mine," he said, turning to her.

"Fine. I get my coat."

"See you later, Ruby."

Ruby watched them whirl away in his red Toyota, her eyes wide under their paddings of flesh, her lips parted. Between their leaving the kitchen, and their climbing into Robert's car, she had, for the first time in her life, fallen deeply and completely in love, in an utter simplicity of loving that saw nothing beyond the radiance cast by the beloved object; where, in the outlying darkness beyond that bright light, vocabularies such as compatibility, reciprocity, practicality, and common sense were rendered alien and meaningless. She loved: That was all she needed to know and all there was to know. His hand where he had—she raised her hand

and touched her hair, slowly. His lips where he had—she raised her hand again and laid it softly against her own lips.

Turning, she walked in a dream through the house, lightly touching everything he had touched. She sat in his chair in the dining room, and leaned back. The wooden bar at her back was as she could imagine his arm to be: strong, supportive, steady as a rock. She climbed the stairs to his room, her breath laboring through her open mouth. He had unpacked a few things: shaving gear, a shirt. She slid his shaving brush over her cheek, let it rest long on her lips; breathed in the scent of his cologne, slipped some between her massive breasts. The shirt was hanging in the closet; she stroked it, letting her fingers linger over the breast, imagining his body beneath the silky material. He must have lain down on the bed for a while: She could see the indentation in the quilt. Quietly, she lay down, closing her eyes, feeling her body sinking into the quilt's softness. This was where he would lie tonight, and he would not know that her body had been here before him. I love you, she told him silently, I love you, I love you. The window was open; he must have opened it when he arrived last night. She rolled from the bed, pressing down with both hands in order to heave the ponderous burden of herself up from the bedding, and stood where he must have stood, her hands gentle on the window handles. Their next-door neighbor was mowing his lawn, and a breeze brought her the dizzying fragrance of cut grass. The leaves of the tall trees were urgent under the breeze, silver-furred in the sunlight, wildly blowing back, bending back wildly together. Their rustling came to her like a distant music, like wild water cascading over rock, like two golden figures hidden deep in grass . . . Still in a dream, she waddled back to her own room. One glowing, growing thought had taken possession, and now all her mind, all the intense warp and weft of her nature, was merging on that one shining thought. The man she loved would be eating here tonight, and it would be her hands and heart that would be creating the meal. Removing two one-hundred dollar bills from the box where she kept her Michelangelo prints, she called a taxi to take her downtown.

It was seven-thirty when she carried in the dinner to them. She was now wearing a brown bag of a dress, for excitement and anxiety had forced such an evacuation of perspiration that she had had to change. Mrs. Lee had exclaimed in surprise at the sight of the gay red tablecloth, the big earthenware jug of country-white daisies and the bottles of chianti. A birthday present to herself, Ruby mumbled, and in honor of the guest's Italian heritage. During the anxious debate with herself that afternoon, she had decided to make him a traditional Italian meal. This idea had swelled irresistibly; it was as if his acceptance of her preparation of dishes from his own ethnic background would also mean that he was accepting of her, that he would be taking her into himself. It would be her way of making herself part of his culture: a world of passion and art, of color and musical syllables bubbling over the tongue. Michelangelo Buonarroti. Roberto Mansini. Roberto, *mi'amore, te amo*. Guided by the instinct of her art, she was moving towards him in the only way she knew. Through the fragrant combinations of fish, meats, vegetables, and herbs, she would be speaking to him her own private language of love.

To whet his appetite, she had prepared Zuppa De Calamari Carciofi, which her Italian cookery book had assured her was a dish guaranteed to rouse the senses: a soup of tender white squid stewed in olive oil, kissed with wine, perfumed with garlic, spangled with glowing wafers of artichoke, and poured over the golden crunch of toasted Italian bread: fresh, lovely, and different, a visual delight of liquid pearls and soft, swirling greens. She served it, her hands trembling, then waited anxiously in the kitchen until she judged it time to return. His response was all she could have wished: He exclaimed when he saw her; he was rolling the tenderness of the squid around his tongue, he was mopping up every last succulent drop, and asking for more. Mrs. Lee was saying, "Delicious, delicious," but Ruby scarcely heard her. Excitedly, she brought in a smoking heap of Gamberi Ai Ferri Come Le Connocchie: fresh crunchy shrimp in their shells, marinated in olive oil, salt, little nipping bites of black pepper, and grilled rapidly. Her cookery book had said that the great pleasure of eating these came from the manner of eating: the picking up of the shrimp and the invasion of the delicate shell with the fingers, the enclosing of the lips around the shrimp, the exploration with the tongue, and the sucking in of the sweet, moist, pink flesh: what the Italians called *"col bacio"*—with a kiss. She waited for this moment from him, and when his lips closed soft and full around the first shrimp, the color rose in her face. With these she served also Farsumauru Il Braciolone: pink petals of veal, stuffed with an assortment of earthy yet spicy sausages, salamis, cheeses, and hard-boiled eggs, slowly pan-roasted in an ambrosial white wine and served aromatic in its own succulent sauce. As an enhancement to the shellfish and meats, she had prepared Carcifini Gratinati: tempting slices of artichoke over-come by butter and parmesan cheese and the love-bite of fra-grant lemon. Melanzanine Con La Mozzarella, a bosomy eggplant whose purple silks had been split in two, cooked slowly in olive oil, garlic, and parsley, the tender flesh caressed by a layer of melted mozzarella: and lastly, Carote Con I Capperi, a brilliant interlude of carrots whose sweetness was pierced and heightened by the tart shock of capers.

Robert, tasting and exclaiming, could not get enough. He ate and ate. Mrs. Lee, on the other hand, had grown strangely quiet. For a while, she watched Ruby waddling in and out of the dining room with her face all aglow; then she asked, "Where did you buy all this, Ruby?"

Ruby could scarcely pay Mrs. Lee any attention. She was moving around in a kind of controlled yet inflamed tension, ev-erything about her receptive to every expression of enjoyment on

Robert's face, to the movements of his hands, busy with the food, to every swallow of each delicious morsel. She replied distractedly that she had bought everything at a delicatessen in the new shopping plaza. Mrs. Lee paused for a moment before murmuring, "That is a long way away . . . Well, I congratulate you, Ruby. You have surpassed yourself this evening."

Ruby forgot her immediately—it was time to bring in the salad: Insalata Di Arancia, a heady concoction of sharp, sweet oranges and cucumbers, tangy with lemon juice and starred with crisp snowflakes of sliced radish, dressed with fresh mint and salt: sharp and cleansing to the palate, preparing the tongue for dessert. With it she served her fragrant homemade rolls of Pane All' Olio, fine-textured, yielding deliciously to the teeth, and she watched tensely as Robert's lips fastened around the golden crust, and opened it into a flower of white and gold.

Originally, she had planned a dessert of Zuppa Inglese to bring the meal to its climax, wanting to place before him some reference to the country from whence her own roots sprang; as if, in this dish, their two cultures, their two selves, might intermingle and become one. Then she had decided that he might prefer something lighter, after all. She had created a rich emulsion of eggs and cream; an ice cream of pure melting lusciousness, yielding, fragrant with vanilla, topped with chocolate-dipped, ruby-red fresh strawberries that exploded their winey flesh into the mouth, each glistening ivory spoonful melting creamily and languidly down the throat, leaving the diner in a state of dreamy ecstasy, the unforgettable gift of it lingering on his tongue.

The meal was an intoxicating, magnificent success. She smiled and smiled as Robert heaped praises upon her. Never, he said, finishing a second cup of her cappuccino, had he ever had such a splendid meal, a meal fit for a prince, for a king! He went on and on, Mrs. Lee nodding beside him, but with her watchful gaze still on Ruby's face. And then a wonderful thing happened, something so totally unlooked and unhoped for, that it left Ruby stammering. He wanted to show his appreciation, he said. It was still reasonably early, and it was, after all, her birthday. If she wished, he would take her to a nightclub, or perhaps the theater, she just had to say the word.

She couldn't believe it, she couldn't believe such a miracle could happen to her. And yet she knew she could not fit into any nightclub or theater seats; her parents had tried a few times before they had all given up . . . Yet here was the man of her dreams actually proposing to spend precious time with her . . . Quickly, before the gift could be taken away from her, she said she would like to go to the midway.

She had finished stacking the dishes in the dishwasher, and now sat in front of her dressing table, staring at the satin-lined box of Helena Rubinstein makeup that Uncle Edward had given her for Christmas two years ago. She had never used it; she never used makeup; she used her dressing table only for dress-making: scissors and thread still lay on the glass top. She wished now that she had taken lessons in makeup, that she had a bigger mirror, that she had asked Mrs. Lee for brighter lighting. The minutes passed. Her fingers were shaking, the fat actually quivering on the backs of her hands. At times she felt that she could hardly breathe. Her first date, and with such a man! She could scarcely bear the happiness that was in her. Timidly, her fingers entered first this jar, then that. And now, at last, she could put on that special dress that she had made on impulse, because the material had been of such a silken ivory that she had been unable to resist it, whether or not the fashion magazines said that large women should always avoid light colors. Her hair was still coiled on top of her head, with some curls just beginning to spill under the richness of their own weight.

"Rapunzel, Rapunzel, let down your hair," she whispered, and reached up for the hairpins.

Her hair fell about her in a scented shining sea that spread the bounteousness of its billows and crests and shadowed hollows of gold down to where her waist should have been. She picked up her hairbrush and began to brush it out, so that her glistening hair foamed about her, so that her hands were lost under a tumult of gold waves, so that her arms and her back, and the back of her chair, were drowned in the fragrant golden storm of her hair.

When, some time later, she hesitated in the doorway of the sitting room, both Robert and Mrs. Lee were silent for a few seconds. Then Mrs. Lee jumped up.

"Oh—your hair, Ruby, your hair!" she cried. She turned to Robert, and for the first time, he saw consternation in the face that was usually so quiet and composed. "Just look at all that glorious hair, Robert," she said, with a catch in her voice. "Beautiful hair, isn't it, Robert, simply beautiful. Beautiful hair."

"Masses of it," Robert said gallantly. "We'll need an extra seat just to hold it all."

He was grateful for the continuing rush of Mrs. Lee's voice as she praised Ruby's hair. Ruby's appearance appalled him. He saw that the folds on her cheeks were multicolored: some sported a sort of suntan powder, against which her nose seemed strangely white; her cheeks carried a high flush of rouge and her mouth was massive in poster-red paint. She had put dark blue stuff on the first roll of fat on her eyelids, and this had begun to intermingle with another fold, and was travelling upwards, giving the impression of invisible hands slowly raising a blindfold. The eyes themselves were beaded in black mascara, and he saw that these beads, which were Ruby's sparse eyelashes, kept hitting both the upper and lower pads of fat around her eyelids as she blinked shyly in the lamplight, and that this mascara, too, was spreading. He could scarcely pay attention to the hair. In that massive white dress, big as a tent, those boatlike shoes, that clumsy makeup, she looked like a terrible inflated joke doll. He was panic-stricken. He had been carried away by the spell of her cooking, but that spell was now broken, and the full import of his invitation came at him like a hard, cold blow: They would be appearing together in public. He forced himself to smile at her. "You know, Ruby," Mrs. Lee cried—and Robert knew that Mrs. Lee was actually gabbling—"you could sell this hair for a profit—no, you could!" Ruby had pitched into excited laughter. "People do sell their hair, they do indeed," Mrs. Lee rushed on, "and blond hair fetches the highest prices, I know it does. I think Ruby could get three hundred dollars for her hair, Robert."

Robert mumbled acquiescence, while Mrs. Lee kept on and on about the marketability of Ruby's hair. Then, suddenly, she stopped short, as if something had just struck her. Quickly, she said, "You can borrow Mr. Lee's limousine, Robert. It is much more comfortable than your Toyota."

"Thanks, I will," he said, immediately catching the vision that flew between them, light as a bird: the Toyota's cramped seats, and the total impossibility of fitting Ruby into them . . .

They neared the midway as the last of the daylight was draining from the sky. A full moon was swelling behind the nearby mountains and spreading its dim silver net over the city. Ruby sat in a daze. The warm air rushed by her, lifting her silky hair and blowing a strand across her cheek in the same manner as the hair on the beautiful model in the Clairol advertisements. She turned her head in the same queenly manner. She was with the man she loved. They were to spend a whole evening to-gether. A sensation was inside her that was intoxicating in its strangeness: She felt she was all enchantment, all mysterious power, all female. Tonight was hers. Nothing could take it away from her.

The midway's grounds were swarming with people, and they joined the crowds wandering among the various rides and booths. Robert led her helplessly past the flying chairs, the bumping cars, the big wheel, the endless rides and amusements that had seats and supports built only for people of average proportions. Even if Ruby sat by herself in a seat built for two, he thought, it was doubtful that the suspended chain or the confining safety belt would be able to contain her weight and bulk. He walked her past long lineups of staring people, speaking to her erratically of this and that, his gaze fixed straight ahead, so that he need not meet those myriads of staring eyes. The feelings her fat aroused in him, the turning heads, the disbelief in those questioning faces, aroused such a wretchedness in him, such a passion to be gone from her, and such a guilt at this passion to be gone from her, that his mouth had gone dry with the strain of it. Again and again he drew his tongue over his lips. He felt that they were on exhibition: that Ruby's fat was its own glaring spotlight, drawing all eyes to them. He found himself urging her more and more to the outer rim of the midway, which had fewer lights, and fewer people. Eventually, they found themselves among booths where, for a successfully thrown dart or ball, one could win a crinoline doll, or a plastic ashtray. Grateful for the dark, for the lack of people, wanting to expurgate the fever of his guilt, he stopped at several of these stalls, piling balls or darts into Ruby's hands, throwing them himself again and again.

She saw his urgent seeking to win a prize for her, and her happiness grew. She did not care whether he won anything for her or not. She had the gift of his presence, and that was enough. Her desire to make love to him, to have him make love to her, was growing as simply and as inevitably as a stream flowing into a river, as a river flowing into the sea. She kept glancing sidewards at him, at his thick fringe of eyelashes, at his mouth . . . Her stomach turned over and melted away when she looked at his mouth, for she had just glimpsed his tongue as he suddenly drew it over his lower lip, and she could already feel the warm moistness of it moving inside her own mouth . . . At his hands, the long, sensitive fingers that would explore and caress . . . At his hips and thighs, outlined under the smooth-fitting jeans, the thighs that would join her to the male weight of him; his entering of her in the sweet contraction and expansion that was the movement of the universe, until his fire exploded in her womb, illuminating all that had previously been darkness to her . . .

Eventually, they came to the western edge of the fair, and here, a metal slide of gigantic proportions raised its structure into the night sky. A staircase of perhaps a hundred steps led to a platform at the top, where a broad lane of metal, perhaps twenty-five feet in width, undulated in gleaming waves to the ground below. At last, here was something in which Ruby could participate. Thankfully, Robert paid for two tickets, lifted two sacking mats, and they began the slow, laborious ascent. Laborious because Ruby quickly became out of breath. The effort of heaving her bulk up step after step! The steps multiplied themselves endlessly; she had to hang on to the handrail, and then use both hands on it to haul her body up yet another step. When eventually they reached the top landing, all her flesh was trembling with the effort, with the gigantic mechanics, the fulcrums, the levers of arms and legs needed to push her weight up one hundred steps.

They had arrived under a superstructure that rose from each side of the slide and formed an arch over their heads. She stumbled to the edge of the safety railing, struggling to control the stentorian noises threatening to drag apart her lungs. She had to get her breath; she had to! She pretended to linger over the view. They were so high above the midway that the only light to reach them here was the light of the moon, and neon bulbs of the concession stalls and amusement rides below them were but encrustations of brilliant coral beneath their feet. Music reached them from a distant loudspeaker, its voice muted by a cool wind that carried with it perfumes of salt and pine. The double row of trolley chairs below them moved in a slow dream from the western edge of the midway to the east, and from the eastern edge back to the west. A sudden rush of wind lifted her moonlit hair and blew it about, so that each long gleaming strand seemed to leap in wild dance. In the distance they could see the shadowed silver pentagram of the Juan de Fuca Strait, edged by embroideries of streetlights, and above that, the dark power of the snowcapped mountains, emerging like crowned warriors out of the earth, and above them again, the moon, riding forward and high over the mountain crests and bringing in its train cavalcades of stars.

She heard Robert murmur, "Beautiful, beautiful," and when she turned to him, her gleaming hair blew across his lips, so that he had to raise both hands in order to lift its richness away. In the wash of moonlight his face was almost featureless: the eyes shadowed, the mouth a dim line. He shook out the two pieces of sacking and arranged them side by side. Silently, as if in ceremony, he handed her onto the mat on his left, and she poised, leaning slightly forward, looking down on the metal lane that flowed in long gleaming curves to the concession stands below. Her feet in their heavy shoes were invisible in the shadow cast by the arch; her dress glimmered silver-white in the moonlight, the upper half of her body was veiled by the spun gold of her hair. He sat down on the mat beside her, leaned sidewards, placed a hand in the small of her back, and pushed.

She was swooping forward into space, weightless, light as a bird, Robert a dark shadow riding beside her. She was riding with him over the glimmering curves as freely as a bird rides the planes of the wind, and at each hill in the metal, she soared lightly into the air, and all her body seemed to expand and open before contracting into the dizziness of the next downward rush. Down and down she flew, and her hair whipped behind her, scattering the moonlight; down and down, and the lights of the midway rushed to meet her, and the music swelled and the heat and the ecstasy of the earth was all about her. The descent stopped all breath; her breath gathered under her breast, then as she approached the last, long curve, and spun towards the landing stage, her mouth opened, and she cried out, sharp and high.

She was dizzy; she was laughing; she was in a tangle of arms and legs, and tangled in the arms and legs of Robert beside her.

"Oh, let's do it again," she cried. "Oh, I want to do it again. It was so lovely!" She heard him laugh indulgently beside her. Triumphant, she dared to take his hand and pull him towards the lineup near the kiosk. "Oh, hurry, hurry," she cried.

The lineup ended in an area beside the Crazy House, beside the two distorting mirrors that were erected outside. She turned, and unexpectedly found herself looking into one of them. A girl looked back at her, a girl with her hair but not with her body. The girl's body was slender, and tall, with a small waist and slim hips. The girl's breasts curved tenderly, and her features were clear; everywhere there were curves, and slenderness, and flowing, feminine lines. This girl, looking back at her in the mirror, was beautiful. She stared, not believing what she saw.

She became aware that Robert was breaking up beside her. He was doubled up with laughter, choking with it, pointing at the second mirror, unable to speak because of the laughter erupting out of him. She looked. Robert was gone. In his place was a squat, gross creature of monstrous proportions. A great head ringed by a neck as big as a truck tire, ballooning chest swallowing up bulging hips and huge belly, hands and face like massive moons . . .

She became very still.

Presently, Robert became aware of her stillness. He stopped laughing, looking at her, puzzled, wiping away tears of laughter from his eyes. Then he caught sight of her reflection in the mirror, and his own reflection mirrored beside it. His expression changed immediately.

"Oh my God!" he said softly.

Her pain was livid in her face, and, beneath it: naked, irrefutable, utterly without artifice, was her desire for him. It was his turn to stare disbelievingly, as if he were seeing her for the very first time. Then he took a small, quick step backwards. It was at that moment that she realized it had not been that he found her fat unimportant: rather, it was that for him, until this moment, her fat had neutered her. She flushed a dark, agonized crimson.

"Oh God," he said again; then, "Ruby, I'm sorry—I'm sorry—truly I'm sorry."

The silence stretched between them.

"Ruby—" he began again, but she made a little convulsive movement with her hand, as if to quiet him. They continued to stand together, not speaking, Ruby's gaze fixed on the ground.

A stone lay near one of the mirrors, gray, misshapen, big as a clenched fist. She went quite still, looking at it.

"Ruby," he said, frightened.

She did not look at him, only kept her eyes fixed on the stone.

"Ruby—Ruby—" he said wretchedly, "would you—would you like to go back home now?"

Again, only silence.

"Ruby," he said. "Ruby, please."

For answer, she turned laboriously away from him, and pushed her fat towards the main gate.

Mrs. Lee was waiting up for them in the sitting room, a big pot of coffee half-empty by her side, several half-smoked cigarettes crowding the ashtray. She had paused rather abruptly after exclaiming that they were back early, then quickly asked if they would like some fresh coffee.

"No, thanks," Robert said. "I—I'd better get to bed. Got to make an early start." He turned to Ruby and said, too heartily, "I'll be leaving about six, so I guess we won't be seeing each other again—"

"What, so soon?" exclaimed Mrs. Lee; then she looked as if she wished she'd kept her mouth shut.

"The traffic," Robert said—again, too heartily. "Thanks again for the wonderful—the truly wonderful meal."

Ruby said—and part of her wondered how odd it was that the voice could sound so calm when all was chaos inside—"You're very welcome. Goodbye."

"I shall get up to speed you on your way—no, I insist," Mrs. Lee said.

"Thank you. Well . . . good night. Goodbye, Ruby." The door closed quietly behind him.

"Do have some coffee with me, Ruby," Mrs. Lee urged.

"No, no thanks, Mrs. Lee. I think I'll go to bed myself now."

"Are you really sure?"

When Ruby nodded, Mrs. Lee stood up and, for the first time, took Ruby's hands within her own. "You know, Mr. Lee and I, we are so happy to have you with us," she declared. "You have made my task of hostess so very easy for me. Whoever gets you gets a treasure, Ruby, a treasure."

"Thank you, Mrs. Lee. That's very kind. I'll say good night now."

"Good night, my dear, and sleep well." Her hands tightened, holding Ruby fast. "Remember what I tell you."

Moonlight was flooding Ruby's room with its antique light. She did not bother to switch on the lamp, but undressed quietly in the dark, folding the trusses and slings of her massive undergarments onto the chair, and hanging the marquee of her dress in the closet. The little jars of the Helena Rubinstein beauty kit glimmered on the dressing table: frail ghosts in the moonlight. Silently, she packed them back into the box, and replaced the box in the bottom drawer, beside the box of Michelangelo prints. Her dressmaking scissors were still on the dressing table, their long, slender blades gleaming in the moonlight like twin swords. She regarded the scissors for a long minute, her face in shadow, her hands tight by her sides. Then her chin lifted; she replaced the scissors in the top drawer, and got out her hairbrush. She brushed and brushed her hair, lifting great handfuls and watching the hairbrush ride down the golden streams. At last she finished, and labored into bed.

She sat for a while, the bedclothes about her knees, watching the moon. Tomorrow, she thought, for the very first time, she would create and name a dish that would be all her very own, forever. She would make it from the delicate white breast of finely ground chicken, mixed and melting into a velvety gelatin base of cream cheese whipped with fresh cream, flavored delicately with one or two herbs, and with just a touch of the vivid shock of lemon to bring the saliva to the tongue. She would mold it into the shape of a bird in flight, possibly a hummingbird: that tiniest and most vulnerable of all the birds, which, even so, pitted its frail yet determined strength against the longest migratory flight of all, from South America to Alaska; living, not on the dross of worms, but on the nectar of flowers. She would decorate this bird with petals and leaves made of stiffly whipped and tinted cream. It would be garlanded at the throat with the fire of the crimson rose and the purity of the white; leaves as green as all the earth would trail from the wings and tail, intermingled with forget-me-nots in shades of blue ranging from the sapphires of a summer sea to blues as deep as the universe itself. On the breast, chosen by herself from the garden, would be one, small, ruby-red flower. She would call this dish "Oiseau au Bijou"— Jeweled Bird.

Quietly, she lifted her hair behind her and lay back, so that in the soft wash of moonlight, her hair lay about her like a carpet of gold.

$\mathcal{L}$oosening Strings or Give Me an 'A'

Ntozake Shange

yes/i listened to Country Joe & The Fish/
   yes/ i howled with Steppenwolf/
yes/Fleetwood Mac was my epiphany/
   & Creedence Clearwater Revival
swept me neath the waters/ Hendrix
my national anthem always/ yes
   Blind Lemon Jefferson & B.B. huddle
by my stage door/ yes Chuck Berry lives
next to me/ yes
   Eric Clapton made me wanna have
     a child named Layla/ yes
Sonny Sharrock drew screams outta me
       Linda can't eclipse/
yes/ i remember My Lai & the Audubob debacle
yes/ Hamza-el-Din is a caracole out my mouth
yes/ i never forgot where i came from &
nobody misses me cuz/
     i never left
in search of a portrait
   of an artist
     as a yng man/
yes i read ULYSSES & he came home
     yes/ oh/ yes
       i know my / Joyce
i cd tell niggah chords meant for me/
yes/ "I'm searchin . . . I'm searchin"/ my Olympics say
Circe, the Scylla the Charybdis,
     any Siren and all the Pentagon

yes / Circe, the Scylla, the Charybdis,
        any Siren and alla the Pentagon
aint kept/ yes/ i say/ aint kept
this one/ yes niggah man/from/ yes
                makin art outta me
yes/
    "i'm gonna love him all over   all over
        & over"
cuz niggahs aint in search of
    we just get discovered
so/ yes
    i must be the New World now/ yes
i'm in tune
oh/ yes/ play me
            pick my colored tones
yes strum my niggah chords
            find my sharps & flats
let em have space
oh/yes oh/yes   i know my Joyce
& Ulysses/ he done come home
yes/ play me now
yes/make me alla that
yes/ i'll be the bottom or i cd just ride
yes / i know my Joyce   & all you gotta say
        is "Give me a 'A' "
            Ahhhhhhhhhhhhhhhhh
yes / Ulysses he done come home
yes / i must be the New World
yes/ Ulysses he done come home
yes/ i must be the New World
yes/ i'm in tune
just/ yes/ oh yes/ just play me
baby/ play me/
        yes/

Prospects of Joy

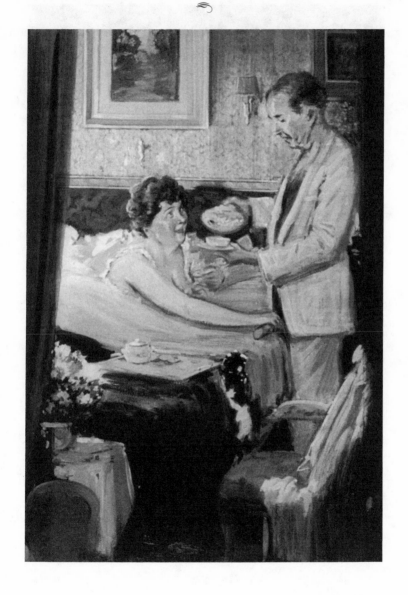

Balcony

Rex Wilder

i.
Her tongue-traveled-upon torso arches
   Inches ahead of the looming
Flicker, in praise of it, like a crowd's
   Progressive ovation, assuming
The lead runner's arrival; or jasmine,
   Anticipating night, blooming—

ii.
If light could slide down your sleeping breasts like water, or the moon
Drop needles on the sea . . . —A mourning dove: *Too soon, soon, soon.*
The perfect note cannot stand on its own.
   Hence memory, the tune.

                    —*Port-la-Galère*

$\mathscr{P}$rospects of Joy

$\backsim$

Charles
Holdefer

Lloyd told the hobo to stay underneath the porch steps. It was Lloyd's idea, and as far as he was concerned, perfectly sensible. Hunger won't just take a walk, he thought. A person's got to have shelter. This is one of my fellow creatures!

Lloyd had been drinking. But he was serious, even if the Iowa horizon bent a little, there was a pleasant gathering in his testicles and above, the stars looked like they were disintegrating. He stood with his head thrown back, teetering slightly, lips parting as one hand pinched himself down low. He felt something approaching peace.

This was ruined, however, when he lowered his gaze. Oh, the hobo's forlorn eyes peeking out from the wooden slats were something he'd never forget!

Earlier, with a skeptical turn of her neck, his wife Jennie had said, "Send him away, Lloyd. I don't trust a hobo who has new shoes."

But Lloyd had already devised a plan. It took only minutes to accomplish. Outside, he pulled out an old mattress from the garage and carefully wedged it beneath the back porch steps. Next he brought the hobo some bread and plums, young carrots from the garden, and told him to be quiet and no one would know he was there.

"You'll be snug as a bug, everybody'll leave you alone."

The hobo swung himself under the edge, then wiggled in deeper, deeper, before reaching up to take the food. His head disappeared.

"That's it, pal," Lloyd told him. "Make yourself at home."

It was a sticky kind of night; the sky was blue black. Cicadas hummed in the catalpa trees.

Then he saw the hobo's eyes in the crack. Such desolation! They blinked at him once, milky, full of doubt, and Lloyd started up the steps, trying to think of something else, anything else, but was aware of a peculiar and uncomfortable point inside him, as if a piece of star had entered his flesh (how or when or why he didn't know) and traveled to a faraway spot in his chest, where now, there could be no doubt, it burned more brightly.

In the kitchen, Jennie asked him, "What is it? You look funny. What's the matter with you?" She stood over the sink with a handful of dirty beets.

"Nothing's the matter with me," he said, stopping abruptly. The piece of star glowed—a crumb with sharp edges, turning—involuntarily he sucked a quick gulp of air.

She tapped the beets against the edge of the sink. She ran water over them, then dropped them in a colander.

"Did you get rid of him?" she asked.

Lloyd pretended not to understand. She would rather not hear the truth, he reasoned, so why tell her? He wouldn't tell her, as a service. He began to hum to himself, "Who's the Prince For You, My Peaches?" He felt no regret for what he'd done. Yes, he'd do it again, in a second!

"Lloyd, did—"

"Yeah, I got rid of him."

After dinner he listened to the radio and drank a Holy Sweet while Jennie heated water on the stove for the dishes. Lloyd was a thin man who looked brittle, who told jokes so Jennie could laugh while she worked. Sometimes, after a couple of Holy Sweets (brandy and last year's white grape juice, a lump of sugar) he sang to her in a dewy tenor, or posed private riddles, exclusively about them—asking, as he drew close, of all the things about her if she knew which he most envied and would like to be, and when she said she didn't know, he ran his tongue along his lower lip and confessed, "The inner seam of your underpants, girlie."

Jennie was laughing right now, as she hefted a log out of the woodbox and into the stove. "Uh—uh—oh!" Lloyd grunted for her. She was an agile woman with a long, strong neck. Lloyd let off talking for a moment and leaned back against the wall to consider the hobo he had hidden under the porch steps. It was a good deed, he thought, but he could not mention it. He would have to hide it in silence where all true good deeds belonged because in the end there was something disturbing about them. In fact, in his experience, a good deed was often such a nuisance (with a voice of its own, stupid in spite of itself, insistent) that it made him contemplate not-so-good deeds, which at least offered more relief.

The stove door clanged shut. Jennie rubbed her nose, blinking. Wood dust made her sneezy.

"Lloyd, do me a favor," she said.

He looked up from his glass, cleared his throat, and sang, "Who's the prince, oh who?"

"Go get me that rinse basin out on the back landing, will you?"

He flexed his arms.

"I could do that," he said.

He wanted a refill. He thought he deserved one. And he wanted to check up on his hobo, so he took the bottle of brandy along with him and stepped out on the porch where he filled his glass with a generosity that lifted his heart. (Thank you, Lloyd. Oh, don't mention it. No, really, thanks—you're one hell of a guy! Well, gee.) A simple act—but what power, sometimes, in simple acts! Neither a good deed nor a bad, this felt like a beauty. Yes, that's what it was, a beauty! And this flush, scratchy-hot up his neck—could that be *hope*? There was no white grape juice out here, no sugar: this Holy Sweet would be holier than most. Lloyd pressed his lips together tight. Mmmrrr. Admittedly, a sip might not douse the piece of star inside (he pictured it flaring, about the size of his thumbnail) but a sip did a tolerable job of harmonizing all things outside. That ought to count for something. Pretty damn good, actually. . . .

of Eros

Lloyd smiled, and it threw him off balance; he took a quick step forward. And suddenly he realized he could hear, from where he stood on the dusty boards, the hobo munching a carrot. He looked over, and saw bright new shoes that shone in the dusk like embers, protruding beyond the edge of the steps. He stepped down and peered beneath the slats, whispering:

"Hey you, don't eat so loud. Judas Priest. Anybody can hear you, I mean it. And pull in your feet—a person can see them a mile off! Right, that's better. Good night, pal."

"Yeah," said a voice from below. "Sweet dreams."

When Lloyd returned to the kitchen she asked him why he'd been gone so long, and where was the basin? He went back and got it, put it in the sink, then leaned one more time against the wall, sipping his drink. It seared his throat nicely. He resumed humming and tried to pick some splinters out of his hands. He worked at the lumberyard from seven to seven. After hours his job seldom entered his conversation, for that would be granting it an even larger part of his life.

What Lloyd resented was not the tasks, he could put up with the lifting, the heat under a tin roof, the scream of the circular saw. (For the last he stuffed toilet paper in his ears, which helped.) No, the real pain was working with Carlton and Ray. The thought of so much of his life spent with them! They told the same joke, all day long.

"Whadya know?" Carlton would ask.

Ray would stop whatever it was he was doing, maybe drop a board—*tonk*—on the ground.

Lloyd shuddered, knowing what came next.

"It takes a big dog to weigh a ton," Ray said.

Carlton thought about this for a moment, rubbing his cheek. He looked over by the fence where the yard dog, Son of a Bitch, lay in the sun. He remarked, "Well, it takes a bigger dog to shit a ton."

He glanced at Lloyd, who pretended not to hear. Even when he left in the toilet paper, the words got through.

Ray turned and called, "Hey, Son of a Bitch!"

Son of a Bitch lifted his head, tilting it to one side. But he didn't come. He never came.

Ray turned back. "Yeah, but it takes an even bigger dog to whip that dog."

Then they threw back their heads and laughed. Every time! It was always the same. Lloyd wondered how long he could bear this, the same words, same pauses, never a change, and the dull heavy way Son of a Bitch lifted his big flat head, then, slowly, lowered it again. He never came! Sometimes Lloyd felt his disgust so overwhelmingly that it was as if the piece of star had dislodged itself from his chest and risen to his brain, burned it out: leaving only light in his skull, illuminating everything with the starkest, yet not to be trusted, clarity, so that he felt he could run out and do something unforgivable, set a public place afire or hurt a small child, perhaps, to get back at them.

He was much better off here at home, with Jennie to talk to. Calmer. The brandy made his hands numb and his words clever, and he spent many enjoyable evenings this way, sipping and picking at his hands, making Jennie laugh. Now he admired her while she worked, and told her, "When you bend over, you are so—I truly mean it—fascinating."

A low chuckle. "I don't know if I'm listening," she said.

Jennie was a deliberate-moving woman with full hips that even in this faded cranberry dress, Lloyd observed, were a subject of considerable consequence, yes, how they jutted so fundamentally! He thought of rubbing his face on those curves. They meant so much! Lloyd was convinced after countless hours of studying them, then thinking about them in spare moments or throughout his workday for solace from Carlton and Ray (here, rubbing his face was not enough—he buried it), that along with the stirring, conspicuous glory of woman's bottomdom was something uniquely hers. Once he'd fallen on his knees behind Jennie and told her so, and she looked back and confirmed, "Yes, that's me all right."

Now Lloyd savored an image of exciting Jennie with relentless, tickly kisses—oh, sneaking from behind, what cunning! A warmth spread through his limbs, better than any dream. "Listen, I got a suggestion," he said in a soft serious voice that made Jennie pause for a second, lift her head as she scrubbed the frying pan. "What is it, Lloyd? What?"

Jennie was tired, the heat from the stove on a summer night was sucking away all her energy. Sometimes Lloyd's words made her laugh, but other times, she preferred to follow her mind down its own path. Even now as she washed dishes she'd enjoyed a recollection of a shimmering lake, where tall birds with backward knees stood nonchalantly in cool water. Delicious! She was a little girl sitting in a rowboat with her straw-hatted father and her dog Clifford. Over the edge of the boat a fish wiggled in the clear water, which also reflected the sky: Clifford trembled, whined, his eyes rimmed in white as if he were deliriously happy or about to die. He barked at the fish in the sky. Jennie's father didn't understand and she laughed and laughed so hard she felt a drop of pee in her underpants.

Jennie scrubbed, chuckling softly at the memory, then Lloyd's words came. She wasn't sure she'd caught them, and told him so. He drew closer, put his hands on her hip. Squeezed.

"You lovely lamb chop. I'm yours."

She shook a plate, then laid it on its face. "Good, Lloyd."

"Come here," he said, bringing his other hand.

"I am here. Do something, give me some cool water for my face. My hands are soapy."

He reached for a tea towel and dipped its corner in cool water, and then, brushing aside sticky strands of her hair with his fingers, wiped across Jennie's forehead. "Yes, Lloyd, that's it," she said. He dipped again and wiped each temple and around the soft borderline of her scalp, leaving no spot untouched. She closed her eyes, and he wiped her eyes, too. There was a pause, in which the sensation of her eyes still lingered on his fingers and he was so caught up in her face it might as well have been his own, because he felt the pleasure, in his fingers—he was certain. Now she nodded (eyes still closed, waiting), so he dipped again and continued down to the bridge of her nose, the hard and hollow of her cheeks, gazing at her, loving this face which seemed so vast, shining with water.

At moments like these Lloyd forgot. He completely forgot anybody else, his anger at others and Son of a Bitch. He even forgot the piece of star the size of his thumbnail. He felt himself too busy with this joy.

She drew a breath, air hissing wet across her teeth.

She lifted her chin so he could get at her neck. He started another corner and wet her all the way around. Gentle lines of pleasure broke around her mouth. "You can't imagine," she said, "how much . . ."

Her voice trailed off, her fingers began to work at her buttons. Lloyd's hand moved farther down, gathering up her dress.

"I do imagine," Lloyd whispered. "I do. We got so many reasons. Let me see you, Jennie, I wanna see you, show me."

She stepped carefully out of her underwear. Lloyd kicked his pants across the room. He wore no underwear. He took a swig of brandy while the radio played snooty clarinet music that excited him. He sauntered around the kitchen. When Jennie stood up straight, he felt a rush of happiness. So lucky! There was nothing else they needed. Her bare breasts pointed, at him, he was sure, so he began to sing.

Oh, I'm the prince
and have been since
forever and evermore,
Oh, I'm the prince . . .

Jennie grinned, giving her stomach a scratch.

"Is that so?" she said. "Well, come on. How 'bout showing me?"

Lloyd took a couple of bobbing steps toward her while she gazed at him, Jack Out of His Box, she called this swollen, ready pink reason that had sprung out of his frame, which on such occasions he seemed to follow around with happy desperation, unable to catch up with it until he brought it to her. Jennie liked the tightly knotted appearance at the base, the plumness, which sometimes purpled with pleasure before her very eyes. How nicely they fit in the cup of her hand!

But just as she was reaching out, suddenly Lloyd stopped, the soles of his bare feet squeaking on the tile. He shook his head.

"What is it?" she asked. "I'll give them back when I'm done, Prince, I promise."

But he didn't even answer. His eyes looked past her. Slowly she turned around—and jumped at the sight of a man at the screen door.

"Wha—!"

His nose was flattened against the wires. Face motionless, staring.

"It's that hobo!" She looked back and forth between the screen and Lloyd. "That hobo you sent away!"

The hobo's face, though cut up into countless pieces by the wire mesh, was recognizable.

Lloyd nodded, licking his lips, straining to collect his thoughts (impose some harmony!) but there was a haze in his head. The Holy Sweets weren't working. He thought angrily: Of all times, why does he come *now*? What the hell does he want? I gave him something to eat. He's got a place to sleep. What's he doing here?

Now the face blinked. The lips moved, and out came a mournful voice:

"It's lonely. Lonely."

Lloyd felt a burning on his face, all over his skin. Without looking at Jennie, he took a step forward, shouted: "Hey, you— get out of here!"

Jennie reached for a chair. She stepped forward too, holding the chair at her side, ready to throw it if the door opened. "Go away!" she yelled.

After a moment of silence the face in the wire shifted, the lips parted.

"I have nothing," the hobo said. "What is there for me? It's lonely."

Lloyd shook his head. He still tasted brandy in his mouth but it was no longer good; it soured on his tongue. He felt like spitting. "You don't belong here," he insisted. "You have to move on. What are you doing?"

But the hobo refused to budge. He pressed his palms against the wires, beseeching. Jennie considered throwing the chair at the door, she wanted to, but decided to save it in case the hobo tried to come in. The mere thought made one of her arms twitch, while Lloyd wondered: Maybe it was the piece of star's fault. Had it made him take in the hobo in the first place—only to punish him after? Was it a malicious star?

"Well I'm not going to put up with any more of this," Jennie said, letting go of her chair to snatch up her dress from the floor. "Even if you're lonely we can't fix that. It's not so simple!" She thrust her arms in her dress, then hastily threw it over her head, pulled it down around her.

"No!" the hobo cried. "No!"

Lloyd saw his pants clinging to a counter, and went over to them.

"No!"

Lloyd stepped into his pants, tucking himself in. With a moan the face pulled away from the screen: a rapid, heavy tread pounded across the porch, then on down the steps.

Lloyd and Jennie looked at each other across the room. They moved to the door, arriving at the same time, and peered out.

No one in sight.

They hesitated, then slowly pushed out onto the porch. The screen door clapped shut behind them.

Dusk. The grass in the backyard smelled cooler now, and patches of air were blackening. Nothing, not a bird, not a bud, moved. Jennie crossed her arms in front of her.

"Cleared out, don't you think?"

Discreetly Lloyd looked past her to the edge of the steps— but didn't see anything. Maybe he *did* run off, he thought. Maybe . . .

"We'll lock up tight tonight," he said loudly.

She looked at him. "Right."

She felt an agreeable stillness, maybe it was the air. "Be a long time before I forget this," she said, shaking her head. Jennie rocked back on her heels, inhaling and smelling the trees. "You know he'll always be out there." She pictured herself and Lloyd, his desperate, ready pink reason and, especially, the moment of reaching out to hold that tight plumness. She laughed softly, conscious of her dress against her skin, which was both pleasant and unpleasant at the same time. She gave herself a squeeze with her arms in front of her, gathering herself up, and desire broke out in her again, a sense of unfinished business.

"Well," she said. She squeezed again, finding a lower edge of a nipple and dragging up on it. She stepped closer, brushing against him with her hip.

Lloyd was looking down at the porch floorboards.

"Let's go in," she told him.

Lloyd's throat tickled, teased, begged for another Holy Sweet, but it was too late for that, he knew, suddenly feeling drunk and even wobbly but taking no pleasure in it.

Jennie released herself for a moment, then pressed once more, this time pinching.

"Come on, baby," she said. "Don't you know what I'm thinking?"

He turned, met her eyes and then one of her hands was sliding, grasping him below. Lloyd's fingers twitched at his sides. As he realized what would happen next, the moment changed and there was anticipation not of tears, not of desire, but of something greater. He gazed at her face. "Yes, Jennie." He was amazed at this prospect of joy. It would simply happen, regardless of the hobo or what one did or didn't do for him, or which lies were known or unknown. It would happen regardless of tomorrow and Son of a Bitch. This fact struck him as both beautiful and horrible: there were sparks from the star.

Wrestling with Angels

Mary Mackey

You meet them in
   the most unlikely places
so at first you may think
they are not angels at all.
But look closely:
their faces are pale
                  or brown
and they shine on you
like suns
their lips are dry
their eyes hot
and their only message
is raw need

the desire of angels
is so completely refined
that it coats their cheeks
like grease
their arms may be strong
or thin
it doesn't matter
for when they have you
in their grip
they can pull your face
to theirs
as easily as if they had
your soul on runners

the first moment
they touch you
is the most terrifying
you can feel their fingers
dig into your shoulders
you can smell the despair
on their breath

sweet as poppies
sour as bitter lemons

their techniques vary.
some will hug you close
and burn you with their
bodies
others will push you away
and then clutch you
suddenly
with sharp clicks
like mousetraps going off
under the bed
still others will lie on
   top of you
until you forget who you
are
but you can always tell
when you are wrestling
with an angel
because just under
   their flesh
you can feel the rusty
edge of your childhood.

as they press you
to the earth
their faces will change
like strips of film
superimposed
you may see your mother
or your father
or an old lover
but whoever it is
it will cause you pain
(the angels know this

and will use it
   against you.
never let them take you
at night
never let them catch you
off balance)

as you struggle,
remember that they too
are vulnerable:
on their backs you will
   find
two hard ridges
just below their
shoulder blades
slippery and sharp
as fish scales
where their wings
were once attached

if you want to win
take a deep breath
seize those ridges
and pull the angel close

the one thing it can't bear
is love

relentless love

that grabs
and hangs on.

My Methodist Grandmother Said

Mary Mackey

My Methodist
grandmother said
that dancing
was adultery
set to music

how right
she was

in that sweet sway
breast to breast and
leg to leg
sin comes into its own

if you have never
waltzed
you can not imagine
the sheer voluptuousness
of it
the light touch
palm to palm
wool and silk
mixed below the waist
the warm breath
of your partner
on your neck
coming quicker
and quicker
the strength of the man
the yielding of the woman

so incorrect
so atavistic
so unspeakably sweet

he moves toward you
and you back away

he pursues you
and with the faintest
pressure
you encourage him
and watch the blood
rush to his face

not a word is spoken
    no one sees this
although it's done in public
in full sight of everyone

you touch
and retreat
meet
and touch again
    in time to the
    music
saying yes
no
yes
no
yes
no
yes

you dance
in a place outside of time
without thinking of your body
in that gentle
rhythmic
careless
almost copulation

one
two
three

one
two
three

the longest
foreplay
in the western
world.

The Extraordinary Member of Carlos Artiga

Joan Frank

People who do not know him treat Carlos as if he were like any man.

He is not like any man.

Carlos Artiga is not tall, but he has a peculiar massiveness, a great solidity. His presence in the room is like the thickened trunk of a fantastic tree. His limbs are dense, bulging; they can crush. He wears his clothing loosely, but the contours surge heavily against the cloth. His skin is rough, like tree bark. His body has endured every manner of physical ordeal, and in exotic response has grown a sort of inuring tissue, head to toe. Yet his hands remain quite small, creamy and smooth as a child's, as do his feet. His face too is smooth, neither young nor old, peering like an ageless bird's.

Carlos Artiga projects a tremendous force, or force field. The only proper way to convey the mightiness, the druggy viscosity of it, is to compare it with a cane fire. If you have lived where sugarcane is burned, you know the pulsing heat and crack of it, rippling and popping with flying cinders and dense sulphurous smoke, heat and choking thickness rising and swelling at some distance from the actual blaze. The closer you come, the more you risk.

Carlos was born in a tropical place where Spanish is spoken, and where the sex of the people swings freely and joyously as the clappers in bells. Where Carlos was born, the air is heavy with scents of waxy raw blossoms and frying meat and sticky liquors of ripening fruit. He was bathed in the salt sea and fed sugary cakes, and later he drank rum, and surrounded by the perfume and talcumy sweat and lilac hair oil of his *tíos* and aunties and cousins, his body's memory swelled with this riot of color and smell. He was a mild and sweet child who came as a young man to my country, and while he has made many friends and had vivid adventures here, beneath his skin, circulating through flesh and organs and sometimes filling his eyes like effervescent juices, he carries the sad and beautiful memories of his infancy in the old land.

Carlos Artiga was bequeathed an unexpected legacy. (No one can pinpoint how it happened. His father and brothers are reasonably physical men, satisfied with themselves in these realms, appreciated by their women, but none extravagantly so.) Between his legs dwells a phenomenon that many will likely never see—perhaps even if they saw, they would not believe; certainly *I* will likely never again view such in this life.

It is magnificent even when it sleeps.

Even then, it makes itself felt. It presses and shifts against his trousers like a lazy dog, kicking in its dreams. One cannot help letting one's eyes drift there, to begin to apprehend and measure its agreeable nature. The creature lifts its head joyfully, stirred by as much as a glance, shamelessly craving the slightest attention. Never did you know such vitality as to feel, even accidentally, the sudden wakefulness of Carlos's member, the bounding, begging, vigorous, insistent pushing and prodding. It seems to be the engine of a larger being, the conductor of a reverberant and unutterable power, as the engine room of a great ocean liner might hum, and palpate.

His member tells Carlos the time. It wakes him, makes him doze, leads him from room to room, demanding its bath and airing. It is his barometer, his metronome, his tutor. If he is ill, it informs him so, and instructs him in methods of care. The size of it—ah. Let us say that the fisted forearm of a large man might not compare in dimension to the fully wakened member of Carlos Artiga. Truly, it is an unnamed wonder of the world, and poor Carlos its shy and weary chaperone. For it troubles him no end, and he sighs frequently with the weight of it.

When it commands release, Carlos has no choice. He will not be able to undertake the day's commerce until the tyrannical member is given its way. And that is when I am often pressed to duty, and I cannot pretend to you that this is a duty I am always pleased to perform. My work is arduous, uncomfortable, requiring great endurance and tricks of breathing. There has only been a bit of blood, but I would be lying to deny that I have suffered. Still, I rush to help him, to do what is needed like a triage nurse, because I have no heart to refuse poor Carlos, seeing how it sorrows him, the burden of serving this voracious master; it is a curse on him, unceasing, a separate function in a separate room that must be attended before he might ever turn to the calmer duties of this world. It exhausts him, and makes him lonely. Who can help Carlos? Who can truly comprehend it? Who else is so imprisoned in his own life, indentured forever to his own insatiable part? Were it up to Carlos, he'd surely prefer to lie floating in a rowboat on a hidden pond, dozing, listening to the *whip-porbula-wheep-weep-weep* of a birdcall, or to press the jewel pastes of watercolors on porous white paper, rendering a purple-yellow iris in the afternoon light, or to sit by the window practicing an ancient air on his wooden lute. The leisurely peace of these pastimes must seem to Carlos luxurious beyond saying, for the extraordinary member of Carlos Artiga is subject to no one. It is lord.

I am fortunate that I need see my suffering friend only twice a year, when business brings him to my city. But each visit looms for me, a grave ordeal. I must prepare well. I must take adequate rest, and exercise and nourishment, allow only serenest thought. I must clean and cook, and drape myself in beautiful vestments, so as to achieve an axis of calm, a plumb line of clarity. I will need all my power to help poor Carlos.

He will arrive at the airport with his customary nervous sweetness, rumpled overcoat draping that tree-trunk torso. I am always touched to see this dear man, shy, pleased, dense as an oak door walking toward me, with the tender, deliberate, careless bravura of any of the thousand others around us on a city day. It makes me ache, and love him more, to recall his burden: He is not like the others. We will embrace fondly, Carlos and I, glad friends reunited, and we will drive somewhere to drink and talk and compare our lives, and at first the time will pass agreeably. But soon enough the talk will falter and sputter as his member begins to knock restlessly between us, hammering, first at him, then at me, knocking and yanking like an overgrown, jealous child growing crosser and crosser. Finally there is no further hope for talk, and exchanging doleful glances, sighing wearily, beleaguered parents to the furious junior, we'll have to rise, and make our way to the hotel.

Oranges and Roses

Ronald Baatz

tonight she didn't know
i was watching her as
in the bathroom she
shaved under her arms
at the sink. somehow
i had managed to open
the door a slit without
her knowing. she
stood there completely
naked under transparent
bulb, and it was strange
how i seemed able to see
every inch of her flesh
without moving my eyes, as
they chose to just come
to a comfortable pause on
the side of her breast.
i was transfixed with the
shadow of breast so cool
and so inviting on the side
of her body. at any second
i expected her sensuous life
to be handed over to me
through the slit in the doorway,
in a small envelope scented
with oranges and roses.
such a moment i could've
smelt coming from across
a lake. and truthfully,
i know she knew i was watching.

i could tell by the way
she concentrated so much under
the arm that was closer to me.
in fact, i don't think she even
shaved under the other arm at all.
and i should know, considering
i was there watching when first
she took off her undershirt.

Orbiting

Bharati Mukherjee

On Thanksgiving morning I'm still in my nightgown thinking of Vic when Dad raps on my apartment door. Who's he rolling joints for, who's he initiating now into the wonders of his inner space? What got me on Vic is remembering last Thanksgiving and his famous cranberry sauce with Grand Marnier, which Dad had interpreted as a sign of permanence in my life. A man who cooks like Vic is ready for other commitments. Dad cannot imagine cooking as self-expression. You cook for someone. Vic's sauce was a sign of his permanent isolation, if you really want to know.

Dad's come to drop off the turkey. It's a seventeen-pounder. Mr. Vitelli knows to reserve a biggish one for us every Thanksgiving and Christmas. But this November what with Danny in the Marines, Uncle Carmine having to be very careful after the bypass, and Vic taking off for outer space as well, we might as well have made do with one of those turkey rolls you pick out of the freezer. And in other years, Mr. Vitelli would not have given us a frozen bird. We were proud of that, our birds were fresh killed. I don't bring this up to Dad.

"Your mama took care of the thawing," Dad says. "She said you wouldn't have room in your Frigidaire."

"You mean Mom said Rindy shouldn't be living in a dump, right?" Mom has the simple, immigrant faith that children should do better than their parents, and her definition of better is comfortingly rigid. Fair enough—I believed it, too. But the fact is all I can afford is this third-floor studio with an art deco shower. The fridge fits under the kitchenette counter. The room has potential. I'm content with that. And I like my job even though it's selling, not designing, jewelry made out of seashells and semiprecious stones out of a boutique in Bellevue Plaza.

Dad shrugs. "You're an adult, Renata." He doesn't try to lower himself into one of my two deck chairs. He was a minor league catcher for a while and his knees went. The fake zebra-skin cushions piled as seats on the rug are out of the question for him. My futon bed folds up into a sofa, but the satin sheets are still lasciviously tangled. My father stands in a slat of sunlight, trying not to look embarrassed.

"Dad, I'd have come to the house and picked it up. You didn't have to make the extra trip out from Verona." A sixty-five-year-old man in wingtips and a Borsalino hugging a wet, heavy bird is so poignant I have to laugh.

"You wouldn't have gotten out of bed until noon, Renata." But Dad smiles. I know what he's saying. He's saying he's retired and he should be able to stay in bed till noon if he wants to, but he can't and he'd rather drive twenty miles with a soggy bird than read the Ledger one more time. Grumbling and scolding are how we deMarcos express love. It's the North Italian way, Dad used to tell Cindi, Danny, and me when we were kids. Sicilians and Calabrians are emotional; we're contained. Actually, he's contained, the way Vic was contained for the most part. Mom's a Calabrian and she was born and raised there. Dad's very American, so Italy's a safe source of pride for him. I once figured it out: his father, Arturo deMarco, was a fifteen-week-old fetus when his mother planted her feet on Ellis Island. Dad, a proud son of North Italy, had one big adventure in his life, besides fighting in the Pacific, and that was marrying a Calabrian peasant. He made it sound as though Mom was a Korean or something, and their marriage was a kind of taming of the West, and that everything about her could be explained as a cultural deficiency. Actually, Vic could talk beautifully about his feelings. He'd brew espresso, pour it into tiny blue pottery cups, and analyze our relationship. I should have listened. I mean really listened. I thought he was talking about us, but I know now he was only talking incessantly about himself. I put too much faith in mail-order nightgowns and bras.

"Your mama wanted me out of the house," Dad goes on. "She didn't used to be like this, Renata."

Renata and Carla are what we were christened. We changed

to Rindy and Cindi in junior high. Danny didn't have to make such leaps, unless you count dropping out of Montclair State and joining the Marines. He was always Danny, or Junior.

I lug the turkey to the kitchen sink where it can drip away at a crazy angle until I have time to deal with it.

"Your mama must have told you girls I've been acting funny since I retired."

"No, Dad, she hasn't said anything about you acting funny." What she *has* said is do we think we ought to call Doc Brunetti and have a chat about Dad? Dad wouldn't have to know. He and Doc Brunetti are, or were, on the same church league bowling team. So is, or was, Vic's dad, Vinny Riccio.

"Your mama thinks a man should have an office to drive to every day. I sat at a desk for thirty-eight years and what did I get? Ask Doc, I'm too embarrassed to say." Dad told me once Doc—his real name was Frankie, though no one ever called him that—had been called Doc since he was six years old and growing up with Dad in Little Italy. There was never a time in his life when Doc wasn't Doc, which made his professional decision very easy. Dad used to say, no one ever called me Adjuster when I was a kid. Why didn't they call me something like Sarge or Teach? Then I would have known better.

I wish I had something breakfasty in my kitchen cupboard to offer him. He wants to stay and talk about Mom, which is the way old married people have. Let's talk about me means: What do you think of Mom? I'll take the turkey over means: When will Rindy settle down? I wish this morning I had bought the Goodwill sofa for ten dollars instead of letting Vic haul off the fancy deck chairs from Fortunoff's. Vic had flash. He'd left Jersey a long time before he actually took off.

"I can make you tea."

"None of that herbal stuff."

We don't talk about Mom, but I know what he's going through. She's just started to find herself. He's not burned out, he's merely stuck. I remember when Mom refused to learn to drive, wouldn't leave the house even to mail a letter. Her litany those days was: when you've spent the first fifteen years of your life in a mountain village, when you remember candles and gaslight and carrying water from a well, not to mention holding in your water at night because of wolves and the unlit outdoor privy, you *like* being housebound.

She used those wolves for all they were worth, as though imaginary wolves still nipped her heels in the Clifton Mall. Before Mom began to find herself and signed up for a class at Paterson, she used to nag Cindi and me about finding the right men. "Men," she said; she wasn't coy, never. Unembarrassed, she'd tell me about her wedding night, about her first sighting of Dad's "thing" ("Land Ho!" Cindi giggled. "Thar she blows!" I chipped in.) and she'd giggle at our word for it, the common word, and she'd use it around us, never around Dad. Mom's peasant, she's earthy but never coarse. If I could get that across to Dad, how I admire it in men or in women, I would feel somehow redeemed of all my little mistakes with them, with men, with myself. Cindi and Brent were married on a cruise ship by the ship's captain. Tony, Vic's older brother, made a play for me my senior year. Tony's solid now. He manages a funeral home but he's invested in crayfish ponds on the side. "You don't even own a dining table." Dad sounds petulant. He uses "even" a lot around me. Not just a judgment, but a comparative judgment. Other people have dining tables. *Lots* of dining tables. He softens it a bit, not wanting to hurt me, wanting more for me to judge him a failure. "We've always had a sit-down dinner, hon."

Okay, so traditions change. This year dinner's potluck. So I don't have real furniture. I eat off stack-up plastic tables as I watch the evening news. I drink red wine and heat a pita bread on the gas burner and wrap it around alfalfa sprouts or green linguine. The Swedish knockdown dresser keeps popping its sides because Vic didn't glue it properly. Swedish engineering, he said, doesn't need glue. Think of Volvos, he said, and Ingmar Bergman. He isn't good with directions that come in four languages. At least he wasn't.

"Trust me, Dad." This isn't the time to spring new lovers on him. "A friend made me a table. It's in the basement."

"How about chairs?" Ah, my good father. He could have said, Friend? What friend?

Marge, my landlady, has all kinds of junky stuff in the basement. "Jorge and I'll bring up what we need. You'd strain your back, Dad." Shot knees, bad back: daily pain but nothing fatal. Not like Carmine.

"Jorge? Is that the new boyfriend?" Shocking him makes me feel good. It would serve him right if Jorge were my new boyfriend. But Jorge is Marge's other roomer. He gives Marge Spanish lessons, and does the heavy cleaning and the yard work. Jorge has family in El Salvador he's hoping to bring up. I haven't met Marge's husband yet. He works on an offshore oil rig in some emirate with a funny name.

"No, Dad." I explain about Jorge. "El Salvador!" he repeats. "That means 'the Savior.'" He passes on the information with a kind of awe. It makes Jorge's homeland, which he's shown me pretty pictures of, seem messy and exotic, at the very rim of human comprehension.

After Dad leaves, I call Cindi, who lives fifteen minutes away on Upper Mountainside Road. She's eleven months younger and almost a natural blond, but we're close. Brent wasn't easy for me to take, not at first. He owns a discount camera and electronics store on Fifty-fourth in Manhattan. Cindi met him through Club Med. They sat on a gorgeous Caribbean beach and talked of hogs. His father is an Amish farmer in Kalona, Iowa. Brent, in spite of the obvious hairpiece and the gold chain, is a rebel. He was born Schwartzendruber, but changed his name to Schwartz. Now no one believes the Brent, either. They call him Bernie on the street and it makes everyone more comfortable. His father's never taken their buggy out of the country.

The first time Vic asked me out, he talked of feminism and

holism and macrobiotics. Then he opened up on cinema and literature, and I was very impressed, as who wouldn't be? Ro, my current lover, is very different. He picked me up in an uptown singles bar that I and sometimes Cindi go to. He bought me a Cinzano and touched my breast in the dark. He was direct, and at the same time weirdly courtly. I took him home though usually I don't, at first. I learned in bed that night that the tall brown drink with the lemon twist he'd been drinking was Tab.

I went back on the singles circuit even though the break with Vic should have made me cautious. Cindi thinks Vic's a romantic. I've told her how it ended. One Sunday morning in March he kissed me awake as usual. He'd brought in the *Times* from the porch and was reading it. I made us some cinnamon rose tea. We had a ritual, starting with the real estate pages, passing remarks on the latest tacky towers. Not for us, we'd say, the view is terrible! No room for the servants, things like that. And our imaginary children's imaginary nanny. "Hi, gorgeous," I said. He is gorgeous, not strong, but showy. He said, "I'm leaving, babe. New Jersey doesn't do it for me anymore." I said, "Okay, so where're we going?" I had an awful job at the time, taking orders for MCI. Vic said, "I didn't say we, babe." So I asked, "You mean it's over? Just like that?" And he said, "Isn't that the best way? No fuss, no hang-ups." Then I got a little whiny. "But *why?*" I wanted to know. But he was macrobiotic in lots of things, including relationships. Yin and yang, hot and sour, green and yellow. "You know, Rindy, there are *places*. You don't fall off the earth when you leave Jersey, you know. Places you see pictures of and read about. Different weathers, different trees, different everything. Places that get the Cubs on cable instead of the Mets." He was into that. For all the sophisticated things he liked to talk about, he was a very local boy. "Vic," I pleaded, "you're crazy. You need help." "I need help because I want to get out of Jersey? You gotta be kidding!" He stood up and for a moment I thought he would do something crazy, like destroy something, or hurt me. "Don't ever call me crazy, got that? And give me the keys to the van."

He took the van. Danny had sold it to me when the Marines sent him overseas. I'd have given it to him anyway, even if he hadn't asked.

"Cindi, I need a turkey roaster," I tell my sister on the phone. "I'll be right over," she says. "The brat's driving me crazy."

"Isn't Franny's visit working out?"

"I could kill her. I think up ways. How does that sound?"

"Why not send her home?" I'm joking. Franny is Brent's twelve-year-old and he's shelled out a lot of dough to lawyers in New Jersey and Florida to work out visitation rights.

"Poor Brent, he feels so divided," Cindi says. "He shouldn't have to take sides."

I want her to ask who my date is for this afternoon, but she doesn't. It's important to me that she like Ro, that Mom and Dad more than tolerate him.

All over the country, I tell myself, women are towing new lovers home to meet their families. Vic is simmering cranberries in somebody's kitchen and explaining yin and yang. I check out the stuffing recipe. The gravy calls for cream and freshly grated nutmeg. Ro brought me six whole nutmegs in a Ziploc bag from his friend, a Pakistani, who runs a spice store in SoHo. The nuts look hard and ugly. I take one out of the bag and sniff it. The aroma's so exotic my head swims. On an impulse I call Ro. The phone rings and rings. He doesn't have his own place yet. He has to crash with friends. He's been in the States three months, maybe less. I let it ring fifteen, sixteen, seventeen times. Finally someone answers. "Yes?" The voice is guarded, the accent obviously foreign even though all I'm hearing is a one-syllable word. Ro has fled here from Kabul. He wants to take classes at NJIT and become an electrical engineer. He says he's lucky his father got him out. A friend of Ro's father, a man called Mumtaz, runs a fried-chicken restaurant in Brooklyn in a neighborhood Ro calls "Little Kabul," though probably no one else has ever noticed. Mr. Mumtaz puts the legal immigrants to work as waiters out front. The illegals hide in a backroom as pluckers and gutters.

"Ro? I miss you. We're eating at three, remember?"

"Who is speaking, please?"

So I fell for the accent, but it isn't a malicious error. I can tell one Afghan tribe from another now, even by looking at them or by their names. I can make out some Pashto words. "Tell Ro it's Rindy. Please? I'm a friend. He wanted me to call this number."

"Not knowing any Ro."

"Hey, wait. Tell him it's Rindy deMarco."

The guy hangs up on me.

I'm crumbling corn bread into a bowl for the stuffing when Cindi honks half of "King Cotton" from the parking apron in the back. Brent bought her the BMW on the gray market and saved a bundle—once discount, always discount—then spent three hundred dollars to put in a horn that beeps a Sousa march. I wave a potato masher at her from the back window. She doesn't get out of the car. Instead she points to the pan in the backseat. I come down, wiping my hands on a dish towel.

"I should stay and help." Cindi sounds ready to cry. But I don't want her with me when Ro calls back.

"You're doing too much already, kiddo." My voice at least sounds comforting. "You promised one veg and the salad."

"I ought to come up and help. That or get drunk." She shifts the stick. When Brent bought her the car, the dealer threw in driving gloves to match the upholstery.

"Get Franny to shred the greens," I call as Cindi backs up the car. "Get her involved."

The phone is ringing in my apartment. I can hear it ring from the second-floor landing. "Ro?"

"You're taking a chance, my treasure. It could have been any other admirer, then where would you be?"

"I don't have any other admirers." Ro is not a conventionally jealous man, not like the types I have known. He's totally unlike any man I have ever known. He wants men to come on to me. Lately when we go to a bar he makes me sit far enough from him so some poor lonely guy thinks I'm looking for action. Ro likes to swagger out of a dark booth as soon as someone buys me a drink. I go along. He comes from a macho culture.

"How else will I know you are as beautiful as I think you are? I would not want an unprized woman," he says. He is asking me for time, I know. In a few more months he'll know I'm something of a catch in my culture, or at least I've never had trouble finding boys. Even Brent Schwartzendruber has begged me to see him alone.

"I'm going to be a little late," Ro says. "I told you about my cousin Abdul, no?"

Ro has three or four cousins that I know of in Manhattan. They're all named Abdul something. When I think of Abdul, I think of a giant black man with goggles on, running down a court. Abdul is the teenage cousin whom immigration officials nabbed as he was gutting chickens in Mumtaz's backroom. Abdul doesn't have the right papers to live and work in this country, and now he's been locked up in a detention center on Varick Street. Ro's afraid Abdul will be deported back to Afghanistan. If that happens, he'll be tortured.

"I have to visit him before I take the DeCamp bus. He's talking nonsense. He's talking of starting a hunger fast."

"A hunger strike! God!" When I'm with Ro I feel I am looking at America through the wrong end of a telescope. He makes it sound like a police state, with sudden raids, papers, detention centers, deportations, and torture and death waiting in the wings. I'm not a political person. Last fall I wore the Ferraro button because she's a woman and Italian.

"Rindy, all night I've been up and awake. All night I think of your splendid breasts. Like clusters of grapes, I think. I am stroking and fondling your grapes this very minute. My talk gets you excited?"

I tell him to test me, please get here before three. I remind him he can't buy his ticket on the bus.

"We got here too early, didn't we?" Dad stands just outside the door to my apartment looking embarrassed. He's in his best dark suit, the one he wears every Thanksgiving and Christmas. This year he can't do up the top button of his jacket.

"Don't be so formal, Dad." I give him a showy hug and pull him indoors so Mom can come in.

"As if your papa ever listens to me!" Mom laughs. But she sits primly on the sofa bed in her velvet cloak, with her tote bag and evening purse on her lap. Before Dad started courting her, she worked as a seamstress. Dad rescued her from a sweatshop. He married down, she married well. That's the family story.

"She told me to rush."

Mom isn't in a mood to squabble. I think she's reached the point of knowing she won't have him forever. There was Carmine, at death's door just a month ago. Anything could happen to Dad. She says, "Renata, look what I made! Crostolis." She lifts a cake tin out of her tote bag. The pan still feels warm. And for dessert, I know, there'll be a jar of super-thick, super-rich Death by Chocolate.

The story about Grandma deMarco, Dad's mama, is that every Thanksgiving she served two full dinners, one American with the roast turkey, candied yams, pumpkin pie, the works, and another with Grandpa's favorite pastas.

Dad relaxes. He appoints himself bartender. "Don't you have more ice cubes, sweetheart?"

I tell him it's good Glenlivet. He shouldn't ruin it with ice,

of Eros

just a touch of water if he must. Dad pours sherry in Vic's pottery espresso cups for his women. Vic made them himself, and I used to think they were perfect blue jewels. Now I see they're lumpy, uneven in color.

"Go change into something pretty before Carla and Brent come." Mom believes in dressing up. Beaded dresses lift her spirits. She's wearing a beaded green dress today.

I take the sherry and vanish behind a four-panel screen, the kind long-legged showgirls change behind in black-and-white movies while their moustached lovers keep talking. My head barely shows above the screen's top, since I'm no long-legged showgirl. My best points, as Ro has said, are my clusters of grapes. Vic found the screen at a country auction in the Adirondacks. It had filled the van. Now I use the panels as a bulletin board and I'm worried Dad'll spot the notice for the next meeting of Amnesty International, which will bother him. He will think the two words stand for draft dodger and communist. I was going to drop my membership, a legacy of Vic, when Ro saw it and approved. Dad goes to the Sons of Italy Anti-Defamation dinners. He met Frank Sinatra at one. He voted for Reagan last time because the Democrats ran an Italian woman.

Instead of a thirties lover, it's my moustached papa talking to me from the other side of the screen. "So where's this dining table?"

"Ro's got the parts in the basement. He'll bring it up, Dad."

I hear them whispering. "Bo? Now she's messing with a Southerner?" and "Shh, it's her business."

I'm just smoothing on my pantyhose when Mom screams for the cops. Dad shouts too, at Mom for her to shut up. It's my fault, I should have warned Ro not to use his key this afternoon. I peek over the screen's top and see my lover the way my parents see him. He's a slight, pretty man with hazel eyes and a tufty moustache, so whom can he intimidate? I've seen Jews and Greeks, not to mention Sons of Italy, darker-skinned than Ro. Poor Ro resorts to his Kabuli prep-school manners.

The Book

"How do you do, madam! Sir! My name is Roashan." Dad moves closer to Ro but doesn't hold out his hand. I can almost read his mind: he speaks. "Come again?" he says, baffled. I cringe as he spells his name. My parents are so parochial. With each letter he does a graceful dip and bow. "Try it syllable by syllable, sir. Then it is not so hard." Mom stares past him at me. The screen doesn't hide me because I've stayed too far in to watch the farce. "Renata, you're wearing only your camisole."

I pull my crewneck over my head, then kiss him. I make the kiss really sexy so they'll know I've slept with this man. Many times. And if he asks me, I will marry him. I had not known that till now. I think my mother guesses.

He's brought flowers: four long-stemmed, stylish purple blossoms in a florist's paper cone. "For you, madam." He glides over the dirty broadloom to Mom, who fills up more than half the sofa bed. "This is my first Thanksgiving dinner, for which I have much to give thanks, no?" "He was born in Afghanistan," I explain. But Dad gets continents wrong. He says, "We saw your famine camps on TV. Well you won't starve this afternoon."

"They smell good," Mom says. "Thank you very much but you shouldn't spend a fortune."

"No, no, madam. What you smell good is my cologne. Flowers in New York have no fragrance."

"His father had a garden estate outside Kabul." I don't want Mom to think he's putting down American flowers, though in fact he is. Along with American fruits, meats, and vegetables. "The Russians bulldozed it," I add.

Dad doesn't want to talk politics. He senses, looking at Ro, this is not the face of Ethiopian starvation. "Well, what'll it be, Roy? Scotch and soda?" I wince. It's not going well.

"Thank you but no. I do not imbibe alcoholic spirits, though I have no objection for you, sir." My lover goes to the fridge and reaches down. He knows just where to find his Tab. My father is quietly livid, staring down at his drink.

In my father's world, grown men bowl in leagues and drink

the best whiskey they can afford. Dad whistles "My Way." He must be under stress. That's his usual self-therapy: how would Francis Albert handle this?

"Muslims have taboos, Dad." Cindi didn't marry a Catholic, so he has no right to be upset about Ro, about us.

"Jews," Dad mutters. "So do Jews." He knows because catty-corner from Vitelli's is a kosher butcher. This isn't the time to parade new words before him, like *halal*, the Muslim kosher. An Italian-American man should be able to live sixty-five years never having heard the word, I can go along with that. Ro, fortunately, is cosmopolitan. Outside of pork and booze, he eats anything else I fix.

Brent and Cindi take forever to come. But finally we hear his MG squeal in the driveway. Ro glides to the front window; he seems to blend with the ficus tree and hanging ferns. Dad and I wait by the door.

"Party time!" Brent shouts as he maneuvers Cindi and Franny ahead of him up three flights of stairs. He looks very much the head of the family, a rich man steeply in debt to keep up appearances, to compete, to head off middle age. He's at that age—and Cindi's nowhere near that age—when people notice the difference and quietly judge it. I know these things from Cindi— I'd never guess it from looking at Brent. If he feels divided, as Cindi says he does, it doesn't show. Misery, anxiety, whatever, show on Cindi though; they bring her cheekbones out. When I'm depressed, my hair looks rough, my skin breaks out. Right now, I'm lustrous.

Brent does a lot of whooping and hugging at the door. He even hugs Dad, who looks grave and funereal like an old-world Italian gentleman because of his outdated, pinched dark suit. Cindi makes straight for the fridge with her casserole of squash and browned marshmallow. Franny just stands in the middle of the room holding two biggish Baggies of salad greens and vinaigrette in an old Dijon mustard jar. Brent actually bought the mustard in Dijon, a story that Ro is bound to hear and not appreciate. Vic was mean enough last year to tell him that he could have gotten it for more or less the same price at the Italian specialty foods store down on Watchung Plaza. Franny doesn't seem to have her own winter clothes. She's wearing Cindi's car coat over a Dolphins sweatshirt. Her mother moved down to Florida the very day the divorce became final. She's got a Walkman tucked into the pocket of her cords.

"You could have trusted me to make the salad dressing at least," I scold my sister.

Franny gives up the Baggies and the jar of dressing to me. She scrutinizes us—Mom, Dad, me, and Ro, especially Ro, as though she can detect something strange about him—but doesn't take off her earphones. A smirk starts twitching her tanned, feral features. I see what she is seeing. Asian men carry their bodies differently, even these famed warriors from the Khyber Pass. Ro doesn't stand like Brent or Dad. His hands hang kind of stiffly from the shoulder joints, and when he moves, his palms are tucked tight against his thighs, his stomach sticks out like a slightly pregnant woman's. Each culture establishes its own manly posture, different ways of claiming space. Ro, hiding among my plants, holds himself in a way that seems both too effeminate and too macho. I hate Franny for what she's doing to me. I am twenty-seven years old, I should be more mature. But I see now how wrong Ro's clothes are. He shows too much white collar and cuff. His shirt and his wool-blend flare-leg pants were made to measure in Kabul. The jacket comes from a discount store on Canal Street, part of a discontinued line of two-trousered suits. I ought to know, I took him there. I want to shake Franny or smash the earphones.

Cindi catches my exasperated look. "Don't pay any attention to her. She's unsociable this weekend. We can't compete with the Depeche Mode."

I intend to compete.

Franny, her eyes very green and very hostile, turns on Brent. "How come she never gets it right, Dad?"

Brent hi-fives his daughter, which embarrasses her more than anyone else in the room. "It's a Howard Jones, hon," Brent tells Cindi. Franny, close to tears, runs to the front window where Ro's been hanging back. She has an ungainly walk for a child whose support payments specify weekly ballet lessons. She bores in on Ro's hidey-hole like Russian artillery. Ro moves back to the perimeter of family intimacy. I have no way of helping yet. I have to set out the dips and Tostitos. Brent and Dad are talking sports, Mom and Cindi are watching the turkey. Dad's going on about the Knicks. He's in despair, so early in the season. He's on his second Scotch. I see Brent try. "What do you think, Roy?" He's doing his best to get my lover involved. "Maybe we'll get lucky, huh? We can always hope for a top draft pick. End up with Patrick Ewing!" Dad brightens. "That guy'll change the game. Just wait and see. He'll fill the lane better than Russell." Brent gets angry, since for some strange Amish reason he's a Celtics fan. So was Vic. "Bird'll make a monkey out of him." He looks to Ro for support.

Ro nods. Even his headshake is foreign. "You are undoubtedly correct, Brent," he says. "I am deferring to your judgment because currently I have not familiarized myself with these practices."

Ro loves squash, but none of my relatives has ever picked up a racket. I want to tell Brent that Ro's skied in St. Moritz, lost a thousand dollars in a casino in Beirut, knows where to buy Havana cigars without getting hijacked. He's sophisticated, he could make monkeys out of us all, but they think he's a retard.

Brent drinks three Scotches to Dad's two; then all three men go down to the basement. Ro and Brent do the carrying, negotiating sharp turns in the stairwell. Dad supervises. There are two trestles and a wide, splintery plywood top. "Try not to take the wall down!" Dad yells.

When they make it back in, the men take off their jackets to assemble the table. Brent's wearing a red lamb's wool turtleneck under his camel hair blazer. Ro unfastens his cuff links—they are 24-karat gold and his father's told him to sell them if funds run low—and pushes up his very white shirtsleeves. There are scars on both arms, scars that bubble against his dark skin, scars like lightning flashes under his thick black hair. Scar tissue on Ro is the color of freshwater pearls. I want to kiss it.

Cindi checks the turkey one more time. "You guys better hurry. We'll be ready to eat in fifteen minutes."

Ro, the future engineer, adjusts the trestles. He's at his best now. He's become quite chatty. From under the plywood top, he's holding forth on the Soviet menace in Kabul. Brent may actually have an idea where Afghanistan is, in a general way, but Dad is lost. He's talking of being arrested for handing out pro-American pamphlets on his campus. Dad stiffens at "arrest" and blanks out the rest. He talks of this "so-called leader," this "criminal" named Babrak Karmal and I hear other buzzwords like Kandahar and Pamir, words that might have been Polish to me a month ago, and I can see even Brent is slightly embarrassed. It's his first exposure to Third World passion. He thought only Americans had informed political opinion—other people staged coups out of spite and misery. It's an unwelcome revelation to him that a reasonably educated and rational man like Ro would die for things that he, Brent, has never heard of and would rather laugh about. Ro was tortured in jail. Franny has taken off her earphones. Electrodes, canes, freezing tanks. He leaves nothing out. Something's gotten into Ro.

Dad looks sick. The meaning of Thanksgiving should not be so explicit. But Ro's in a daze. He goes on about how—*inshallah* —his father, once a rich landlord, had stashed away enough to bribe a guard, sneak him out of this cell, and hide him for four months in a tunnel dug under a servant's adobe hut until a forged American visa could be bought. Franny's eyes are wide, Dad joins Mom on the sofa bed, shaking his head. Jail, bribes, forged, what is this? I can read his mind. "For six days I must orbit one international airport to another," Ro is saying. "The main trick is having a valid ticket, that way the airline has to carry you, even if the country won't take you in, Colombo, Seoul, Bombay, Geneva, Frankfurt, I know too too well the transit lounges of many airports. We travel the world with our gym bags and prayer rugs, unrolling them in the transit lounges. The better airports have special rooms."

Brent tries to ease Dad's pain. "Say, buddy," he jokes, "you wouldn't be ripping us off, would you?"

Ro snakes his slender body from under the makeshift table. He hasn't been watching the effect of his monologue. "I am a working man," he says stiffly. I have seen his special permit. He's one of the lucky ones, though it might not last. He's saving for NJIT. Meantime he's gutting chickens to pay for room and board in Little Kabul. He describes the gutting process. His face is transformed as he sticks his fist into imaginary roasters and grabs for gizzards, pulls out the squishy stuff. He takes an Afghan dagger out of the pocket of his pants. You'd never guess, he looks like such a victim. "This," he says, eyes glinting. "This is all I need."

"Cool," Franny says.

"Time to eat," Mom shouts. "I made the gravy with the nutmeg as you said, Renata."

I lead Dad to the head of the table. "Everyone else sit where you want to."

Franny picks out the chair next to Ro before I can put Cindi there. I want Cindi to know him, I want her as an ally.

Dad tests the blade of the carving knife. Mom put the knife where Dad always sits when she set the table. He takes his thumb off the blade and pushes the switch. "That noise makes me feel good."

But I carry in the platter with the turkey and place it in front of Ro. "I want you to carve," I say.

He brings out his dagger all over again. Franny is practically licking his fingers. "You mean this is a professional job?"

We stare fascinated as my lover slashes and slices, swiftly, confidently, at the huge, browned, juicy breast. The dagger scoops out flesh.

Now I am the one in a daze. I am seeing Ro's naked body as though for the first time, his nicked, scarred, burned body. In his body, the blemishes seem embedded, more beautiful, like wood. I am seeing character made manifest. I am seeing Brent and Dad for the first time, too. They have their little scars, things they're proud of, football injuries and bowling elbows they brag about. Our scars are so innocent; they are invisible and come to us from roughhousing gone too far. Ro hates to talk about his scars. If I trace the puckered tissue on his left thigh and ask "How, Ro?" he becomes shy, dismissive: a pack of dogs attacked him when he was a boy. The skin on his back is speckled and lumpy from burns, but when I ask he laughs. A crazy villager whacked him with a burning stick for cheekiness, he explains. He's ashamed that he comes from a culture of pain.

The turkey is reduced to a drying, whitened skeleton. On our plates, the slices are symmetrical, elegant. I realize all in a rush how much I love this man with his blemished, tortured body. I will give him citizenship if he asks. Vic was beautiful, but Vic was self-sufficient. Ro's my chance to heal the world.

I shall teach him how to walk like an American, how to dress like Brent but better, how to fill up a room as Dad does instead of melting and blending but sticking out in the Afghan way. In spite of the funny way he holds himself and the funny way he moves his head from side to side when he wants to say yes, Ro is Clint Eastwood, scarred hero and survivor. Dad and Brent are children. I realize Ro's the only circumcised man I've slept with.

Mom asks, "Why are you grinning like that, Renata?"

Salt in the Afternoon

Marge Piercy

The room is a conch shell
and echoing in it, the blood
rushes in the ears,
the surf of desire sliding in
on the warm beach.

The room is the shell of the moon
snail, gorgeous predator
whose shell winds round and round
the color of moonshine
on your pumping back.

The bed is a slipper shell
on which we rock, opaline
and pearled with light sweat,
two great deep currents
colliding into white water.

The clam shell opens.
The oyster is eaten.
The squid shoots its white ink.
Now there is nothing but warm
salt puddles on the flats.

The Medicine Woman's Daughter

Anita Endrezze

A charm to keep you part of the whole

May the white bark be nine times your mother
May my burnished cheeks be twice sun-daughters
May the apple that divides seeds into simple stars
   be the multiple of your life
May my breasts be the marigolds in your night garden
May the dark broom that is your shadow be a memorial
   to your father
May you live between my thighs and in my heart
May lapwings rise at your feet from every crossroad
May I be in between your two hands the way sky is
   the center of beech dreams
May our love be the mystery of the wind and the soul's
   duration
May your life be as charmed, as strong, as the single
   white rose blooming in snowy circles

𝒩otes on the Contributors

Sigmund Abeles received his MFA from Columbia University in 1957 and, after twenty-seven years of teaching art while making art, is now in the studio full time. Together with his wife Anne and son Max (both artists), he has recently moved to New York City after three decades in New Hampshire. Much of his current work is "driven by the incomprehensible question, 'What's it like to be retired?' " He's also observed "a new element of illogical content that has to be a result of Manhattan-mania."

Elizabeth Alexander has published recently in *Poetry* and *Kenyon Review* and is the author of *The Venus Hottentot* (University of Virginia, 1990) and *Body of Life* (forthcoming).

James Clark Anderson manages the Magnolia Bookshop in Augusta, Georgia. His poems have appeared in such journals as *Poetry*, *Yarrow*, and *Calliope*.

Jancis M. Andrews was born in England and lives in Vancouver, Canada. She ran away from school when she was 14, re-entered ninth grade at 36, and received her BFA in Creative Writing from the University of British Columbia at 53. Her first collection of stories, *Rapunzel, Rapunzel, Let Down Your Hair*, was published in 1993 by CaCaNaDaDaDa Press (Vancouver).

Nin Andrews's poems and stories have appeared in many journals, including *The Paris Review, Michigan Review Quarterly*, and *Denver Quarterly*. Her first book, *The Book of Orgasms*, was published by Asylum Arts in 1994.

Ronald Baatz has published three chapbooks of poetry, including *All the Days Are* (Tideline Press) and *Strange Breakfast* (Permanent Press). He lives in upstate New York, where he recently "moved even farther out into the country" and earns his living "working for Cornell University in unexpected ways."

Michel Bernard was born in southern France and currently resides in Paris.

Nick Bozanic is the author of *The Long Drive Home* (Anhinga Press, 1990), a collection of poems. He teaches at the Interlochen Arts Academy in northern Michigan.

Angela Carter was the author of eleven novels, including *Nights at the Circus* (Viking, 1985), three collections of stories, and the screenplay for *The Company of Wolves*. As in "Peter and the Wolf," her short fiction often took a familiar theme and turned it into a sophisticated and erotic contemporary tale. She died in 1992.

Stephen Corey is associated editor of *The Georgia Review*. He has published six collections of poetry, most recently *All These Lands You Call One Country* (University of Missouri Press, 1992), for which he was named Georgia Author of the Year in Poetry by the Georgia Council of Writers and Journalists.

Steven DaGama divides his time between Canada and Cuyahoga Falls, Ohio. He has published five collections of poetry, and his work has been widely translated. He is also an artist, working in crayon and pen and ink. A deluxe limited edition of his poems and drawings, in portfolio boxes handmade by Canadian artist Robert Abuda, was published in spring 1994.

Rachel Guido deVries directs the Community Writers Project in Syracuse, New York, where she also teaches creative writing at the Humanistic Studies Center of Syracuse University. She is the author of a novel, *Tender Warriors* (Firebrand, 1986). Her second book of poems, *How to Sing to a Dago*, will be published by Guernica Editions in 1995.

Lee Durkee was born in Hawaii and raised in Mississippi. He is a recipient of the Henfield Award and has held writing fellowships at Syracuse University and the University of Arkansas. Currently living in Colchester, Vermont, he is finishing a novel "that could use a good agent."

Anita Endrezze is half Yaqui Indian and half Rumanian, Italian, and Yugoslavian. Her work has appeared in many books and journals, including the *Anthology of 20th Century Native American Poets* (Harper & Row), and has been translated into five languages. She is also a painter and storyteller.

Louise Erdrich lives in New Hampshire with her husband Michael Dorris. She has published two volumes of poetry and five novels, including the National Book Critics Circle Award–winning *Love Medicine* (Holt, 1984) and, most recently, *The Bingo Palace* (HarperCollins, 1994).

Kathy Evans lives on a houseboat in Sausalito, California, and has received writing grants from the California Arts Council, the Headlands Center for the Arts, and the Witter Bynner Foundation. Her first book of poems, *Imagination Comes to Breakfast*, was published by Signature Press in 1992.

Diane Frank is the author of three books of poetry. A San Francisco transplant in the Midwest, Diane is known for writing exotic poems about cows. Her forthcoming book, *Letters from a Sacred Mountain Place*, was inspired by a 250-mile trek in the Himalayas.

Joan Frank was "born to New Yorkers in Phoenix" and has traveled in West Africa, Tahiti, Hawaii, and Europe. Her short fiction and essays have appeared in such journals as *Kansas Quarterly* and *Chicago Review*.

Samuel Green is the author of seven collections of poetry, most recently *Vertebrae* (Eastern Washington University Press). With Sally, his wife and partner of 24 years, he is editor and copublisher of Brooding Heron Press. They live in a log house on an isolated island off the northwest coast of Washington State.

Jane Hirshfield's most recent poetry collections are *The October Palace* (HarperCollins, 1994) and *Of Gravity & Angels* (Wesleyan, 1988). She has also edited *Women in Praise of the Sacred* (HarperCollins, 1994) and cotranslated *The Ink Dark Moon* (Scribners, 1988), a volume of ancient Japanese poetry.

Charles Holdefer lives in La Rochelle, France. His work has appeared in *New England Review*, *North American Review*, and *Paris Transcontinental*. He is currently completing a novel.

Karen Lee Hones lives in San Francisco.

Mikhail Horowitz is the author of *Big League Poets* (City Lights) and *The Opus of Everything in Nothing Flat* (Outloud/Red Hill). The most consistently vilified performance poet in the Hudson Valley, his day gig is cultural czar for the weekly *Woodstock* (yes, *that* Woodstock) *Times*.

Teresa Jordan has published a memoir, *Riding the White Horse Home* (Vintage, 1994), as well as an oral history, *Cowgirls: Women of the American West* (University of Nebraska, 1992). She's also edited two collections of women's writing about the West, *Graining the Mare* and *The Stories that Shape Us*. A 1994 NEA Literary Fellowship recipient, she lives with her husband in rural Nevada.

Galway Kinnell is State Poet of Vermont and teaches at New York University. Among his works are the novel *Black Light* (North Point, 1980) and, most recently, *Three Books* (Houghton Mifflin, 1993). A former MacArthur Fellow, his 1982 volume *Selected Poems* won both the National Book Award and the Pulitzer Prize.

Betty LaDuke has traveled extensively in Third World countries, and her numerous publications include *Campaneras: Women, Art & Social Change in Latin America* (City Lights) and *Africa Through the Eyes of Women Artists* (Africa World Press). She teaches art at Southern Oregon State College in Ashland.

Dorianne Laux was born in Augusta, Maine, and is of Irish, French, and Algonquin heritage. Her first book, *Awake* (BOA Editions, 1990), was a Bay Area Book Reviewers' Award Nominee. Her second collection, *What We Carry*, was published by BOA in 1994.

Mary Mackey has written six novels, including *The Year the Horses Came* and *The Horses at the Gate* (both Harper San Francisco) and four books of poetry. Her most recent poetry collection is *The Dear Dance of Eros* (Fjord Press, Seattle). From 1989 to 1992 she served as president of the West Coast branch of PEN American Center.

David Mamet is a playwright, poet, screenwriter, and director. His works include the plays *Sexual Perversity in Chicago*,

Oleanna, and *The Cryptogram*, the screenplays for such films as *The Verdict* and *The Untouchables*, and, most recently, his first novel, *The Village* (Little Brown).

Carole Maso is the author of four novels, *Ghost Dance, The Art Lover, AVA,* and, most recently, *The American Woman in the Chinese Hat* (Dalkey Archive, 1994), which incorporates the story included here.

Stephen Minot teaches creative writing at the University of California, Riverside, though he and his wife "migrate between California and Maine." His stories have appeared in a wide range of journals and have been reprinted in both the *O. Henry Prize Stories* and *Best American Short Stories* series. His books include several novels and a collection of stories, *Crossings* (University of Illinois).

Bharati Mukherjee was born in India and currently teaches at the University of California at Berkeley. Her novels include *Jasmine, The Wife,* and *The Holder of the World* (Knopf, 1993). She is working on a screenplay of "Orbiting."

Christopher Noel has written numerous short stories and one novel, *Hazard and the Five Delights* (Knopf, 1988).

D. Nurkse's books of poetry include *Voices Over Water* (Graywolf), *Staggered Lights* (Owl Creek), and *Shadow Wars* (Hanging Loose Press). He has also written widely on human rights.

Mayumi Oda was born to a Buddhist family in a suburb of Tokyo and now resides in California, where she continues to practice Zen. Her work has been shown widely in the United States, Europe, and Japan. She is the author of *Goddesses* (Volcano Press).

Sharon Olds teaches poetry and writing at New York University. Her second book, *The Dead and the Living* (Knopf), won the National Book Critics Circle Award for 1983. Her most recent collection is *The Father* (Knopf, 1992).

Robert Patierno lives with his wife and three children in Dallastown, Pennsylvania, and teaches drawing, painting, and printmaking at the Pennsylvania School of Art and Design. His work, ranging from landscapes to the human figure, has been influenced by Chardin, Breughel, Bosch, and Goya.

Stephen John Phillips teaches photography at the Maryland Institute College of Art. His work has been published in *Zoom, American Photographer*, and *High Fashion Tokyo,* among others, and is in the collections of the National Museum of American Art, the Corcoran Gallery, and the Baltimore Museum.

Marge Piercy is the author of eleven volumes of poetry and ten novels, most recently *The Longings of Women* (Fawcett, 1994). She has also edited an anthology of contemporary American women's poetry, *Early Ripening* (Pandora, 1987).

Lily Pond, when not gardening, birdwatching, or cleaning the pond, is often found editing or designing *Yellow Silk,* which she also publishes. She feels that any culture that doesn't include the erotic in its legitimate literature is doomed to make more war than it does love.

Donald Rawley has published four volumes of poetry, including *Duende* (1994). The title story of his forthcoming collection, *Slow Dance on the Fault Line,* first appeared in *Yellow Silk* and is being produced as a motion picture.

Carson Reed is a Denver-based journalist, historian, writer, and poet. Author of four volumes of poetry, including *Avante*

Gourd and *Tie Up the Strong Man*, he says "Speaking in Tongues" was written to be performed and "owes an equal debt to Lewis Carroll and Jimmy Swaggart."

Anthony Robbins lives in Monroe, Louisiana, with his wife, Jackie, and their daughter, Genevieve. His first book, *On the Tropic of Time*, is forthcoming from Lynx House Press. "Wonderland" is from his unpublished manuscript, *The Votive Flesh*, parts of which have appeared in *Sulfer*, *Temblor*, *New Directions*, and other journals.

Richard A. Russo was guest editor for Issue 24 of *Yellow Silk*. He has also co-edited a previous anthology, *Yellow Silk: Erotic Arts and Letters* (Harmony, 1990), as well as a collection of dream texts and articles entitled *Dreams Are Wiser Than Men* (North Atlantic, 1987). He writes fiction under the name Richard Cornell.

Andra St. Ivanyi was born and raised in Saudi Arabia by expatriate parents and is currently working in the film industry in Los Angeles. Her work has been published in *Cream City Review*, *Icarus*, and *Sun Dog* and includes a one-act play produced off-Broadway in 1993.

Jan Saudek was born and lives in Prague. Working in a cellar studio, his models are often members of his family, close friends, or even himself. A collection of his work, *Love, Life, Death & Other Such Trifles*, was published in Europe in 1990.

Ntozake Shange was Heavyweight Poetry Champion of the World at the Poetry Circus in Taos, New Mexico (1991–1993). A writer and performance artist, her books include a novel, *Betsy Brown* (1985), a collection of poems, *Nappy Edges* (1978), and the "choreopoem," *for colored girls who have considered suicide/when the rainbow is enuf* (1975). Her newest work is the novel *Liliane: Resurrection of the Daughter* (St. Martin's, 1994).

Jim Sorcic was born in Milwaukee and had a normal childhood "the way Jim Stark in *Rebel Without a Cause* had a 'normal' childhood." "Walking In, Watching You" was written for his first wife, who left him for another woman. His second collection of poems, *Johnnie Panic and His Fantastic Circus of Fear* (Morgan Press, 1994) documents that experience.

Tony Speirs was born in Washington State while Eisenhower was still president. Around the time Johnson stepped in, he moved with his family to the Bay Area, where he rode out subsequent administrations. He currently lives and paints in Berkeley, California.

Martin M. Stone was born in Ohio and lived in Toronto for seven years before moving to Marietta, Georgia, where he has been since 1968. He has taught at the Atlanta College of Art. The work included here is from his *Parthenogenesis* series.

Theresa Vinciguerra founded the Sacramento Poetry Center in 1979 and served as its director until 1985. Her work has appeared in numerous journals and two anthologies, *The Dreambook: Writings by Italian American Women* (Shocken, 1985) and *Landing Signals: An Anthology of Sacramento Poets* (Sacramento Poetry Center, 1986).

Sarah Brown Weitzman won an NEA Fellowship in 1984 and has published over two hundred poems in such journals as *Abraxas, Poet & Critic*, and *Kansas Quarterly*.

Tom Whalen is the author of *Elongated Figures* (Red Dust), *The Camel's Back* (Portals Press), and the forthcoming *A Newcom-*

er's Guide to the Afterlife (a collaboration with Daniel Quinn).

Rex Wilder is a former director of the Poetry Society of America in Los Angeles, which sponsored the acclaimed "Act of the Poet" series at the Chateau Marmont. His work has appeared in *Poetry*, *The Nation*, *The Georgia Review*, and other journals. "Severine Between Marriages," which first appeared in *Yellow Silk*, was a Pushcart Notable Poem of 1993.

Ira Wood is the author of two novels, *The Kitchen Man* (1987) and *Going Public* (1991). He gives workshops and readings across the country and lives on Cape Cod with his wife, the poet and novelist Marge Piercy.

Robert Wrigley lives with his wife and children at Omega Bend, near Rattlesnake Point on the Clearwater River in Idaho. His most recent book is *What My Father Believed* (University of Illinois Press, 1991).

Richard C. Zimler lives in Porto, Portugal, with his lover, Alex. His first novel, *The Last Kabbalist of Lisbon*, was published in 1994 by Editores of Lisbon (in translation). He received a 1994 NEA Fellowship in Fiction and recently edited a special supplement for *Puerto del Sol*, featuring prose, poetry, and art from Portugal.

Bob Zordani teaches English at Seton Academy in South Holland, Illinois, and is the author of two chapbooks, *Last Resort* and *My Funny Barbeque*. An avid fisherman as well as a poet who has published widely in literary journals, his rewards from fishing are much greater than his awards for poetry.